Reading, Learning, Teaching

Barbara Kingsolver

confronting the Text, confronting the World

P. L. Thomas
General Editor

Vol. 1

PETER LANG
New York • Washington, D.C./Baltimore • Bern
Frankfurt am Main • Berlin • Brussels • Vienna • Oxford

P. L. Thomas

Reading, Learning, Teaching
Barbara Kingsolver

PETER LANG
New York • Washington, D.C./Baltimore • Bern
Frankfurt am Main • Berlin • Brussels • Vienna • Oxford

Library of Congress Cataloging-in-Publication Data

Thomas, P. L. (Paul Lee).
Reading, learning, teaching Barbara Kingsolver / P. L. Thomas.
p. cm. — (Confronting the text, confronting the world; vol. 1)
Includes bibliographical references and index.
1. Kingsolver, Barbara—Criticism and interpretation. 2. Feminism and literature—United States—History—20th century. 3. Women and literature—United States—History—20th century. 4. Political fiction, American—History and criticism.
5. Feminist fiction, American—History and criticism.
6. Kingsolver, Barbara—Study and teaching. I. Title.
PS3561.I496Z925 813'.54—dc22 2005010233
ISBN 0-8204-7923-3
ISSN 1556-8288

Bibliographic information published by **Die Deutsche Bibliothek**.
Die Deutsche Bibliothek lists this publication in the "Deutsche Nationalbibliografie"; detailed bibliographic data is available on the Internet at http://dnb.ddb.de/.

Cover design by Lisa Barfield

275 Seventh Avenue, 28th Floor, New York, NY 10001
www.peterlangusa.com

Table of Contents

Acknowledgments

Writing is an act of discovery—this truism has crossed my lips countless times as I have spoken to my students and to teachers during the daunting task of teaching someone else to write. This book has been one of the most vivid verifications of that belief. It started as one book for another publisher but begged until I allowed it to become this book for this publisher. I was simply a vehicle for its finding its way into print.

I taught high school English and worked as an adjunct instructor of English and education classes at the undergraduate and graduate level for eighteen years before making the switch to being a full-time professor of education. I suspect that twenty or thirty years from now, at some point when I have been an education professor longer than I was an English teacher, I will still say that I *am* an English teacher. This book is very much an extension of that and of my other two permanent afflictions—avid reader and driven writer.

What has made the writing of this book extra special has been both my love and admiration for the writing of Barbara Kingsolver and the help and guidance offered me by many of my colleagues, peers, and friends. This list will surely leave someone out, but I want to acknowledge all who helped this work directly and indirectly come to fruition:

- The outstanding and dedicated English teachers of Dorman High School (Spartanburg, SC)—Renee Cline, Heather Loftis, and David Revan—for their patience and the use of their classrooms and the input of their expertise and their wonderful students.

- The input and classrooms offered by my former Furman students and current early career teachers—Megan Alexander (Berea High School, Greenville, SC), Ann Claire Felts (JL Mann High School, Greenville, SC).
- The input and classroom of a graduate student and wonderful middle school English teacher—Kim Long (Hillcrest Middle School, Greenville, SC).
- The feedback, encouragement, and patience of a wide range of people who read this work in its many forms—Carol Jago, Zarina Hock, Kris Harrill, Brandon Shoemaker, and Doris Paez.
- The support and faith of the Lang editors—Joe Kincheloe, Chris Myers, and Phyllis Korper.
- The support, input, and willingness to read my work by many of my friends and colleagues who help me immeasurably with this and other works—Scott Henderson, Ed Welchel, Denise Crockett, George Lipscomb, and Mike Svec.
- The patience, faith, tolerance, and love of my wife, Fran, and my daughter, Jessica.

Ultimately, I want to acknowledge readers and writers, students and teachers—all whom I have known and all who love this as I do.

Introduction

Confronting the Text, Confronting the World

What brings any of us to the words of a writer—words that slip inside us and feel at home? For me, the journey to Barbara Kingsolver has been an embarrassing one because I let a great deal of time slip by after my students and friends said to me, "You *have* to read her." It's the same sort of embarrassment I feel for having let so much time pass before I returned to Kurt Vonnegut—rereading everything he has written and knowing that his work meant something to me that could not be put properly into words. That, too, is how I feel about the writing of Barbara Kingsolver.

Eventually, I picked up Kingsolver's novels and began in fits and starts; even after I read some of her work, the click didn't happen right away.

Then, of course, it *happened.*

I believe it was during *Animal Dreams*—or possibly *Pigs in Heaven*—that I fell in love with the work of Kingsolver, the worlds of Kingsolver, the confrontations of Kingsolver. The confrontations she presented to me. From that day on, I began to recommend her work to every student I taught, every friend I have; I guess I became a *Poisonwood Bible*-thumper, of sorts—the kind I am certain would make Kingsolver herself smile, or possibly wince.

"This is the dilemma upon whose horns I've built my house: I want to know, and to write, about the places where disparate points of view rub together—the spaces between," Kingsolver (1995) writes in "The Spaces Between" (p. 154). Within this brief passage is the seed of what drives me to write this book so that more teachers will read

Kingsolver's writing and, most of all, more students will read her as well and feel themselves rattled by the "spaces between," where ideas and people and beliefs all "rub together," sparking the friction of life. Kingsolver as a human, as a woman, and as a writer is fascinated by the dilemma of living and ever mindful of "disparate points of view"—knowing that those views inevitably "rub together." And these are the confrontations of teaching and learning that we cannot ignore.

And for me, that is the stuff of art, what makes writing beautiful, and the stuff of learning. Children deserve few things more than slipping into the fiction, the essays, and the poetry of Kingsolver as she weaves the world around them and forces them to struggle against the dozens of strands of her verbal web.

Literature and teaching are powerful things that we must not take lightly. Kingsolver takes very little lightly—not the topics she explores and not the craft with which she writes. Bringing her work into the classroom and placing it in the hands of students, as I will explore in this book, can fulfill the huge array of needs we address as ELA teachers—from challenging our students as growing readers to inspiring them as writers to expanding their perceptions of this world as young adults.

As ELA teachers we are under enormous pressures, many of which are detrimental to our fulfilling the literacy needs of our students. Kingsolver's own works drift often into our field of teaching—from her essay recalling the impact a librarian, Truman Richey, had on her life to her main character in *Animal Dreams* falling into a year as a teacher and instilling in her students a moral imperative to learn and to act. Along with her concern for teaching and learning, she is openly an advocate for children.

With this in mind, I believe we have moral obligations as teachers of literacy that call for us to resist the misguided political pressures we feel and remain true to language and learning in our classrooms. As I will discuss in the following chapters, that moral obligation to act is at the heart of Kingsolver's work, and it can invigorate both us as teachers and our students when we find ways to teach the works of Barbara Kingsolver in the ELA classroom.

• • •

Many years ago, I sat among my Advanced Placement English and Literature class discussing the selection of poetry they had read the night before. This particular day comes easily to mind because I began telling the class the most outlandish, most unsupportable interpretations of one poem that a reasonable person could fabricate.

The students obediently jotted down most of what I said in the margins of their textbooks. Not a single question. Not a single challenge.

The next day I confessed and asked why no one had said a word in protest. Possibly more troubling than their silence and compliance the day before was their inability even to explain their own intellectual passivity. This group was very bright and exceptionally literate, but they were also *good students.*

In American classrooms, good students are nothing if not compliant—very quiet and very eager to absorb in order to repeat the required answers when requested (Scheele, 2004). In my more cynical moods, I refer to seasoned students as "intellectual zombies," and I blame many of our traditional practices in schools for the condition—not the nature of children, not the deterioration of culture. And therein lies the motivation for this book.

While many aspects of American education have remained virtually unchanged for over a century, teachers today do face a certain raised intensity concerning some of the more harmful practices—prescriptive lesson planning, teacher-centered instruction, high-stakes testing, national and state standards, and potentially catastrophic accountability measures. Because of federal mandates such as No Child Left Behind (NCLB), our schools are often hostile to the genuine pleasure, passion, and uncertainty that can and should accompany teaching and learning, particularly teaching and learning with literature. Above all else, our schools value compliance by both teachers and students. There are to be no confrontations among people—or among ideas.

Yet if literature (all art, in fact) is anything, it is *confrontational.* Kafka (1979), in a letter to Oskar Pollak, wrote that "[a] book must be the axe for the frozen sea inside us" (p. 290). For him, literature confronted the paralysis that life imposed on him. Interestingly, Ernst Pawell (1984) states simply about Kafka: "He hated school" (p. 26). For me, there is a profound connection here. Our traditional approaches to school—stressing standardization, silence, analysis, quantification (Thomas, 2004), and objectivity—work directly in opposition to the very nature of literature, the heart of English classrooms, confrontation. Kafka's metaphor of the sea fits well the belief I hold about the nature of Self and of teaching and learning; the sea is an ever-moving, ever-evolving thing that is defined by its movement and constant change. Once frozen, it loses its nature.

This book will offer an opportunity for teachers and students to *confront* "the frozen sea inside us," inside our schools, and inside our literature and writing curriculums through the varied writings of Kingsolver. Literature can restore life and living to the classroom and to both teachers and students. Those encounters will take the form of confronting assumptions about learning theory and educational psychology broadly along with reading, literature, writing, instruction, and assessment within the classroom. But exploring Kingsolver will also ask teachers and students to confront the world, to confront concepts often held so sacred that they are never reconsidered, thus allowed to wilt—capitalism, democracy, freedom, ecology, war, peace, human dignity, and more, for example.

Confronting the English Classroom

Those of us who enter classrooms most days as teachers of English might feel our minds click "off" when we are faced with terminology such as "critical pedagogy" or "educational psychology"—especially if we pick up a book hoping it will help us bring something new and exciting into the daily workings of our classes, into our daily lives and those of our students. Before we turn directly to exploring the work of Kingsolver, however, I believe it is important that we explore as practically as possible how this literary exploration can and should be an avenue to greater critical awareness by both teachers and students.

In the broader context, the discussion in the following chapter is supported by my own evolving theory and practice in terms of pedagogy (teaching) and educational psychology (how humans learn, how free humans *must learn*). Embedded in this introduction and in the chapters to follow is my own argument that our English classes must be guided by critical pedagogy (Kincheloe, 2004) and a new postformal vision of educational psychology (Steinberg, Kincheloe, & Hinchey, 1999). See the appendix for a more fully developed discussion of critical pedagogy and postformalism.

The content of our English classes, the literature we choose to explore, can serve us as teachers as much as it does our students. Let's look first at reframing the pedagogy of our classes, the "how" of our teaching. This exploration of Kingsolver will be grounded in the emancipatory potential of education (Freire, 1993) as a way to confront the traditional assumptions of teaching and learning that often paralyze both teachers and students.

Whether coming to Kingsolver for the first time or reexamining her work, teachers can use this opportunity to confront issues of curriculum, instruction, and assessment *in* the English classroom. For most of us, our concerns are directly tied to the daily acts of teaching English. The nature of daily routines can lead to a stasis, a paralysis in teaching, just as it can for students.

This book offers an opportunity to bring a new author into the classroom, an opportunity to expand the use of an author in the classroom, or the opportunity to revisit an author in the classroom. I would argue that many of our practices we implement in our classes need that same revision—a re-*visioning* that we often ask students to undergo when they are analyzing text or writing for our classes. The practices we need to confront in those classes include how we address reading, genres, and literature, how we assign and teach writing, and how we assess both reading and writing.

I would like to offer some avenues to reconsidering the teaching we do in English classes, but I am not claiming to have definite answers to those reconsiderations—although I am suggesting that anyone with monolithic answers is quite probably making a serious mistake. Part of the theory behind postformalism is that confronting and questioning are vital practices, but answers tend to be relative and temporal, approaches that may and will change as time passes. Emerson argues that we should speak loudly those things we believe, although we should be prepared to speak loudly tomorrow in direct contradiction to today's claim: "Speak what you think now in hard words and to-morrow speak what to-morrow thinks in hard words again, though it contradict everything you said to-day" (Emerson, 1981, p. 146). Dewey (Dewey, 1938; Ryan, 1997) offered a similar argument, suggesting that we work as teachers with "warranted assertions" (his postmodern view of science). A warranted assertion entails taking action based on the evidence available at the time (thus the action is "warranted"), but that action can and should shift in future actions as the evidence evolves, changes, grows.

At the secondary and college levels of teaching English, there are some typical characteristics of how we address reading, literature, and genres both in the classroom and in standardized testing. Before discussing those are more fully, let's look at Table 1:

Table 1. Addressing Reading, Literature, and Genre

	Reading	Literature	Genres
Classroom—Curriculum, instruction, and assessment	Teachers expect that students enter secondary and college classrooms as capable or even advanced readers.	Classroom approaches to literature are primarily concerned with analyzing literature to arrive at meaning.	Curriculum values fiction, drama, and poetry over nonfiction genres.
Standardized testing	Reading passages precede multiple-choice questions that primarily assess details and inferences identified by the reader.	Reading passages precede multiple-choice questions that primarily assess literary analysis of passages for the identification of technique and meaning.	Nonfiction excerpts are valued over fiction, drama, and poetry (except in Advanced Placement tests in English).

Although how we actually address the reading aspects and the writing aspects of teaching English may vary, both components are highly interrelated and holistic. I will discuss how the traditional approaches in English courses look beside approaches informed by critical pedagogy and postformal thought. Now, let's add to Table 1 a brief set of distinctions about how we address composition (writing) and surface features (grammar, mechanics, and usage) in the classroom and in standardized testing in Table 2.

Table 2. Addressing Composition and Surface Features

	Composition (Writing)	Surface Features
Classroom—Curriculum, instruction, and assessment	Essay assignments are primarily template assignments that prescribe essay form and the content of the composition; the writing process is often prescribed as well as a linear step-by-step process.	Students learn and are assessed on issues of grammar, mechanics, and usage in isolated ways, in their own compositions, and through editing of the writing of others (grammar texts, worksheets, etc.).
Standardized testing	Essays are often prompted, often require only one draft, and often are limited to very brief amounts of time; the composition is occasionally connected to a reading passage as well.	Tests of surface features ask students to identify or edit sample passages provided for them through multiple-choice formats.

In our experiences as students of literature and in our work as English teachers, we have a great deal of experience with literature *as the goal of instruction.* In high school and college English courses, students study a text or a work of literature with some direct assessment of that text or literature culminating the experience. The student is expected to know details from the text and is expected to be able to analyze and evaluate the text (often analysis and evaluations are *provided for them* by the teacher). A shift that seems appropriate is viewing the reading of text and of works of literature as *avenues* to learning and understanding—not goals. Let's look at an example of each, considering how the approaches at the curricular, instructional, and assessment levels deal with student reading, literature, and genres along with how that literature-driven instruction connects with our teaching and assessment of composition and surface features. (Giving a broad description of a typical situation always risks oversimplifying the situation, thus distorting the quality of the point being made. With that acknowledgment, I will describe *holistically* what I have seen as a typical pattern for the traditional teaching and assessment performed in a literature-driven English class, noting that they are quite similar in essential ways at the secondary and college levels.)

The Traditional Classroom-Literature as the Goal

The class is assigned *The Scarlet Letter;* the choice of that assignment is probably determined at a departmental level and standardized across a level of course work (junior English for secondary students or freshman composition for college students). Occasionally, books are provided for students though they may be asked or allowed to purchase individual copies. Students in varying percentages read the entire book, read part of the book, read materials *about* the book (*Cliff's Notes,* for example), or read none of the book. Teachers often provide reading guides or require students to maintain reading journals in an effort to encourage students to read the text. Teachers might also implement periodic pop quizzes and announced tests to hold student accountable for their own reading. During classroom instruction, teachers tend to directly tell students all that the student need to know about the novel, often guided by the teacher's own knowledge of the test student will take. After the teacher covers the novel, students may take a selected-response test, a created-response test, or be asked to complete an essay on the novel (in the essay assignment, students are provided a template for the essay form and the content of the essay). This slightly distorted model is grounded in assumptions about behaviorism and the technical aspects of teaching and learning. If we look closely at this, we see that the literature study is highly text oriented and teacher centered—the goal being that the teacher transfers a set body of knowledge about the novel to the students in a unified way.

The Critical Classroom—Literature as an Avenue

The class is required to choose and read a novel by an American author. The teacher explains the process for selecting the novel and asks students to express how and why they selected the novels they did. The teacher either introduces students to or reviews for the students scholarly explorations of literature; students are then asked to read and respond to the novel in a variety of ways with the teacher working as a mentor for each student as he or she creates his or her own project that revolves around the novel. Primarily, all of the work and all of the decisions are shifted to the student with the teacher providing expertise and support for the process. The final assessments revolve around students performing their understanding of the novel as a reflection of their understanding of the *process*—not the details or interpretations of any specific novel. If the situation of the teacher precluded being able to allow each student to choose a unique novel to study and all of the class had to study *The Scarlet Letter* (a common situation), the final assessment would have students apply the process they learned from exploring *The Scarlet Letter* to a new situation—possibly having students write an original analysis of a passage by Nathaniel Hawthorne, a passage *not* from *The Scarlet Letter.*

While these examples are brief and oversimplified, they give us a framework for the more fully explored assignments and assessments that will be discussed in the following chapters. Essentially, we will confront the teacher-centered and text-centered practices that make literature the *goal* of instruction and assessment in order to suggest that the English class begin to move toward student-centered and process-centered practices. Power and engagement in the learning process are shifted to the learner, in other words, creating a more authentic and more empowering experience that values process along with product.

Confronting the World

If we begin to confront how we teach, how we view the teaching and learning dynamic, and how we view the teaching and assessing of reading and writing in high school and college English course, then what becomes the larger goals of our classrooms? For me, the beauty of teaching English is that *through* literature and writing we offer students (and ourselves) the opportunity to confront ourselves and our world. Those big concepts that we face will force us to explore and reexamine some of the most significant questions of life and some of the most entrenched assumptions of our living—capitalism, democracy, freedom, ecology, war, peace, human dignity, and such.

Ultimately, we will begin to create an English classroom where the free exchange of ideas is most pervasive process that teachers and students undertake as we grow and change together—without predetermined destinations. The English classroom that confronts the world is a radical classroom; it involves risk for teachers and students alike. But when we ask and when we wrestle with ideas and when we allow ourselves to act through our reflection, we are experiencing authentic learning and we are moving ever closer to the promise of democracy and the hope of social justice.

As Paulo Freire might argue, the English classroom must avoid becoming a place where students acquire the knowledge of their teachers and become a place of learning through reading, writing, speaking, and listening—acts that make us uniquely human.

• • •

"To write novels, to design a museum, to teach fourth-graders about history—all these enterprises require the interpretation of other lives," Kingsolver (1995) states in "The Spaces Between" (p. 153). And so we will begin Chapter One with an interpretation of Barbara Kingsolver's life and work.

Chapter Two will look at the essay—both the reading of Kingsolver's nonfiction and the writing of essays by students in school. The next three chapters will cover the use of three of Kingsolver's novels in English (and other) classes—*The Bean Trees* (Chapter Three), *The Poisonwood Bible* (Chapter Four), and *Prodigal Summer* (Chapter Five). Finally, Chapter Six looks at Kingsolver's only collection of poetry to date, a bilingual series of poems titled, *Another America/Otra America.*

Woven through the chapters will be several related approaches to Kingsolver—**Entry Points, Connections**, and **Student Insight**. Entry Points will offer brief works such as poems, songs, essays, and short stories that can serve to open a lesson or unit on a longer Kingsolver work. The Connections provide examples of related works (novels, essays, short stories, poems, movies) that can be taught in conjunction with Kingsolver, as part of a larger unit including Kingsolver, or as a follow-up unit to a Kingsolver unit. Student Insight sections include actual student work samples from lessons on Kingsolver in the many classrooms acknowledged in the Acknowldgements.

Chapter One

Barbara Kingsolver—Confronting the Politics of It All

"Small change, small wonders—these are the currency of my endurance and ultimately of my life," Kingsolver (2002, p. 21) explains in the opening and title chapter of Small Wonder as she along with the entire world wrestles with a post-9/11 existence—whether we want to or not—and so I will begin here to offer a glimpse into the life of Barbara Kingsolver and the broad tendencies of her work to provide a foundation for moving beyond reading and studying her work to teaching her work. When we are teaching literature, when the focus of our teaching and learning is the writing, the details of a writer's life are always problematic. The details of Kingsolver's life are most often revealed in her essays and her poetry, but her fiction tends to reflect the ideas and beliefs of her life, while only rarely and loosely depending on the facts of her biography (DeMarr, 1999; Wagner-Martin, 2004).

I have read Kingsolver now as a devoted reader, as a teacher, and as a literary critic. Those experiences have pulled me deeper and deeper into her work. I cannot claim to know her; we have never met and we have never spoken. But moving from her fiction, where I came to know what she *believes,* to her nonfiction and poetry, where she revealed some of the details of her life, has convinced me that we need to know these details of her life, at least in a broad sense, and we need to share this with our students.

Confronting the Politics of Living

During the Gulf War under George H. W. Bush's administration, many of us displayed either the flag or an antiwar ribbon depending on our view of the war. Barbara Kingsolver moved from the United States to the Canary Islands with her first husband and daughter to protest that war (DeMarr, 1999). Although I will deal with the facts of her life briefly here, I will try to offer those details that show Kingsolver as a political writer and as a woman of strong conviction (Wagner-Martin, 2004). Life is never as simple or "cause and effect" as biography may make it seem, but I think we can be sure that many moments of Kingsolver's life, at least in their accumulation, help us to better understand the writer she has become so far. Although Kingsolver has built a guarded private life as a highly successful writer, critical works (DeMarr, 1999) and a recent biography (Wagner-Martin, 2004) provide insight into the details of her life that do seem relevant for readers, students, and teachers.

Kingsolver herself speaks often about and relies heavily on her Kentucky roots—born on April 8, 1955, in rural surroundings to parents who instilled in her a keen sensitivity to class discrepancies. Her father was a doctor, whose work seems to have exposed her to socioeconomic and racial segregation and inequity (DeMarr, 1999). Some of her essays reveal that Kingsolver was a somewhat self-conscious young woman who found a great deal of comfort in literature. She writes about being rather tall and having little luck with boys well into high school.

Her sense of not belonging seems to have fueled her desire to flee her hometown for college—as much as an escape as an intellectual pursuit. At DePauw University in Indiana, she majored in biology after beginning college as a music major (Wagner-Martin, 2004); her knowledge of and interest in science are cornerstones of her fiction, nonfiction, and poetry. After college, she moved abroad before returning to the United States for a master's degree, again in science, at the University of Arizona. DeMarr (1999) explains that even though Kingsolver eventually lost interest in completing her doctoral degree, her years spent at college shaped many of the beliefs that would soon come to life in her writing—a concern for ecology and a love of nature, a sense of social justice, a drive to be a writer, a political view of the world.

Other details of her life have surfaced in her essays as well. Kingsolver's first marriage ended in divorce; currently, she is remarried, having a daughter from each marriage. The trauma of her marriage ending and of being a single mother for a time surfaces in her essays; further her concern for *motherhood* pervades much of her fiction. Additional trauma came earlier in her life when she was the victim of date rape in college. With both the rape and the end of her first marriage, it seems that Kingsolver's work often expresses a great sensitivity to situations of powerlessness (DeMarr, 1999; Wagner-Martin, 2004).

Possibly the greatest details of Kingsolver's life for both us as readers and as teachers are the places she has lived. It is difficult to separate her views from the *places* of her life. Born in Kentucky and then attending college in the Midwest, Kingsolver has established Tucson, Arizona, as sort of the nexus of her fictional universe, but her well-traveled life has included the Canary Islands, Africa, the Caribbean, France, and many places in between. David King Dunaway notes that Kingsolver embodies "a meeting of Southern and Southwest identities" because of "her preoccupation with society . . . and her . . . attention to land and diverse people" (Wagner-Martin, 2004, p. x). As I will explore in the following chapters, Kingsolver's work projects a strong sense of place.

The eclectic nature of her travels and her homes parallels the eclectic nature of her interests and talents. Trained as a scientist, Kingsolver also is a skilled musician and, obviously, a gifted writer, though her path to being a novelist has been unusual. Kingsolver has noted being influenced by writers such as Doris Lessing and Francine Prose, under whom Kingsolver took a course in creative writing (DeMarr, 1999; Wagner-Martin, 2004). Though she worked at times as a journalist, it seems that writing was born to her, almost unexpectedly. Her first novel, *The Bean Trees,* was written during her first pregnancy seemingly as a strategy to overcome the insomnia and discomfort of pregnancy. Even with the publication of her book of poetry, *Another America,* Kingsolver admits that it took her many years to consider herself a novelist—and she still refrains from calling herself a poet.

Wagner-Martin (2004) acknowledges that Kingsolver's formative years and the window her writing provides to her life show that she embodies characteristics of low self-esteem—from her feeling of failing with boys as a young girl to her fears concerning her looks to her own references to herself as "stupid" though she graduated from high school as valedictorian and from college with honors (p. 23). College and young womanhood brought her into a world of Marxist and feminist thought along with social activism and eventually a wandering away from the academic and professional life of a scientist and toward the self-sustained life of a novelist who received a one-million-dollar advance from her publisher.

Confronting the Politics of Writing

DeMarr (1999) identifies two key elements of Kingsolver, the writer: She openly embraces the role of political writer, and she begins her writing with a question, applying her training as a scientist to her calling as a writer. While many writers shun the label "political," Kingsolver relishes the role (Wagner-Martin, 2004). As well, she seems to write to discover—"her process of writing leads to new insights" (DeMarr, 1999, p. 7)—although she herself is a woman of strong convictions. The result is that Kingsolver's writing deals complexly with the big ideas that humans face—making her works valuable vehicles for learning in our classrooms. While many of her characters and her own voice in her essays express certain unwavering beliefs, her work refrains from preaching though it always provokes, again, ideal sources for teaching and learning. The essentially questioning nature of her writing fits well with the need for inquiry in teaching and learning.

As of the writing of this book, Kingsolver has published five novels, a collection of short stories, a nonfiction book, two books of collected essays, and a book of poetry, which includes Spanish translations along with her original verse. I will not look at using all of Kingsolver's work in our classes, but I do feel that the vast majority of her work is suitable in varying contexts and for many purposes in the high school and college English classroom (along with courses in science, religion, history, and others). As I discuss strategies applied to a specific work, I realize that such strategies will fit many other of her works as well. Kingsolver's writing also is suitable for the classroom since she works in many genres, notably providing a wealth of engaging nonfiction to integrate into our explorations as readers and writers.

Kingsolver's first novel, *The Bean Trees* (1988), will be the focus of Chapter Three. It is a complex and rich novel that is also highly accessible for readers of all abilities in high school. Taylor Greer is the main character of the novel who flees her home town and her actual name (Marietta). During her trip West, she becomes the surrogate mother of an abandoned Native-American baby, who is misnamed Turtle (in that Taylor simply creates the name "Turtle" since she has no idea of the child's given name), before settling in Tucson, Arizona. The complications of her move and of becoming an accidental mother drive this novel. As mentioned earlier, Kingsolver wrote this first novel in a closet as she suffered from insomnia during her pregnancy; Wagner-Martin (2004) notes that Kingsolver learned four lessons from this first attempt at being a novelist—an affection for the voice of her main character, an attachment to Tucson, a belief in the need to express something she had wanted to express all her life, and an embracing of her own optimism and sense of humor (pp. 60–61).

ENTRY POINTS

Kingsolver's short story, "Homeland" (*Homeland and Other Stories*), can serve as an excellent entry point to *The Bean Trees.* Often, a shorter work such as a short story, a poem, or a song can help create interest, background knowledge, or content information for students who are going to study a longer work in class or as an outside assignment. "Homeland" shares with *The Bean Trees* a focus on characters rooted in

Kentucky and conflicts rising from Cherokee ancestry. *The Bean Trees* has a pivotal scene involving a night-blooming desert flower and a subplot concerning American involvement in Guatemala (personified by the characters Estevan and Esperanza); both the flower image and the political issue of Guatemala can be introduced through the alternative rock group REM's song "Flowers of Guatemala" (*Lifes Rich Pageant* [sic]). This activity will be explored more fully in Chapter Three.

Critics consider her second novel, *Animal Dreams* (1990), "the first one she wrote purposely after beginning to consider herself a professional writer of fiction" (DeMarr, 1999, p. 69). As a result, in some ways, this novel is more solidly crafted. The story involves a complex and interesting pair of sisters, Codi and Hallie Noline, with Codi carrying the narration along with their father, Homer, who is drifting into the grips of Alzheimer's disease. Codi returns to her hometown after failing to complete her work to be a doctor as well. Her sister travels to Central America as an act of political activism, and Codi takes a temporary job as a science teacher. Codi remains somewhat detached during the novels but cannot avoid reuniting with a high school lover and deeply impacting both her students and the locals to become politically active themselves; Wagner-Martin (2004) explains that Kingsolver used her first nonfiction work, *Holding the Line,* as the basis for her fictional protests in *Animal Dreams* (p. 81). As with most of her works, this novel deals extensively with multicultural themes involving Mexican Americans and Native Americans.

ENTRY POINT

Animal Dreams includes a subplot with a characteristic Kingsolver concern for political activism; in the novel, the main character, Codi, organizes the locals into the Stitch and Bitch Club to fight the pollution of local waters by a mining company. "Cuyahoga," also by REM (*Lifes Rich Pageant*), is an excellent song dealing with the actual polluting of the Cuyahoga River, which spontaneously caught on fire from industrial pollution. Another entry point is Kingsolver's own essay, "Careful What You Let in the Door" (*High Tide*), in which she explores the larger issue of the use of violence in writing (DeMarr, 1999). *Animal Dreams* can serve as an excellent novel for any high school or college English class because of its high level of craft and its vibrant consideration of themes—nature, relationships, parents and children, disease, teaching and learning, among others. These entry points might work well when assigning *Animal Dreams* for extracurricular study or as an extension to another exploration of Kingsolver's works.

Kingsolver looked back at her first novel and felt many of the questions she raised remained unexplored when she created the world of Taylor and Turtle. The result was her third novel, *Pigs in Heaven* (1993). Continuing the story of Taylor Greer and her adopted daughter, Turtle, the novel wrestles with the problem that adoption entails: Which should be honored, the desires of the individual (personified by Taylor, who loves Turtle as much as if she were biologically hers) or the values of the community (represented by Annawake Fourkiller, a lawyer representing the Native-American culture and its claim that Turtle belongs to her people)? Of course, complicating this conflict is the interests of a child, Turtle.

ENTRY POINT

"Indian Boarding School: The Runaways" by Louise Erdrich (1984) is a vivid poem that explores the tension between cultures, specifically Native American and American, that Kingsolver often explores, such as in the conflict personified by Taylor Greer and Annawake Fourkiller of *Pigs in Heaven.* Using Erdrich's poem to introduce students to the conflict can provide a framework for the much more fully explored conflict in Kingsolver's novel. Erdrich's poem also addresses concerns about how we perceive "home," includes a reference to the Turtle Mountains (echoing the name of the child in Kingsolver's novel), considers that act of running away (as Taylor experiences), and looks at the world through the eyes of children. These thematic concerns parallel well with *Pigs in Heaven;* as well, Erdrich's poem is beautifully realized in its use of imagery and language.

CONNECTIONS

Many students will find themselves deeply concerned with the characters in *The Bean Trees,* which leads to a natural continuation of *Pigs in Heaven.* This pairing can be done in class or as an outside assignment. Chapter Three will touch briefly on the possibilities of connecting these companion novels.

The Poisonwood Bible (1998) stands both as an incredibly complex and beautifully realized novel and as the work that moved Kingsolver to the level of popular authors, garnering status as a *New York Times* bestseller and a selection for Oprah's Book Club. Inspired somewhat by Joseph Conrad's *Heart of Darkness* and reminiscent in many respects of Alice

Walker's *The Color Purple* and William Faulkner's *As I Lay Dying,* this novel follows a family of missionaries, the Prices, to the Congo, primarily during the mid-1900s. The novel's narration switches among the women of the novel—the mother, Orleanna, and the four daughters, Rachel, Leah, Adah, and Ruth May. The father, Nathan, is a powerful force in the novel, but "he does not speak for himself" (DeMarr, 1999, p. 125). This novel is incredibly rich and ambitious. Chapter Four will look at some of the many opportunities that this novel offers for English courses or for classes dealing with religion, philosophy, history, or geography.

Prodigal Summer appeared in late 2000. This novel, set in the southern Appalachia of Virginia, weaves together three intriguing stories that share strong connections with nature. The dominant story revolves around Deanna Wolfe and her hesitant but engrossing relationship with Eddie Bondo, which interrupts her solitary life on Zebulon Mountain. The story of Lusa Landowski and Cole Widener unfolds in the valley below Deanna; this tragic relationship explores issues of marriage as Lusa finds herself in charge of Cole's farm. The third story revolves around two elderly characters who are antagonistic neighbors—Garnett Walker and Nannie Rawley. Both the motifs and stories of this novel are rich and may stand as her most mature work to date; this novel is possibly best suited for advanced high school and college consideration because of its sexual content, making it unique among Kingsolver's novels. Chapter Five looks at teaching *Prodigal Summer* along with the novel's ability to provide us teachers an opportunity to renew ourselves as readers and lovers of literature.

The remainder of Kingsolver's work includes a collection of short stories, *Homeland and Other Stories;* a collection of poetry (all poems in both the original English and Spanish translation), *Another America/Otra America;* and two outstanding collections of essays, *High Tide in Tucson: Essays from Now or Never* and *Small Wonder.*

Kingsolver's fame revolves primarily around her work as a novelist, but few are aware of her collection of short stories, *Homeland and Other Stories* (1989). Throughout this book, I will note a few stories that can be used in conjunction with other Kingsolver works, but these stories are quite accessible in the classroom because of their relative brevity (as compared to novels). These stories explore themes common to Kingsolver (which I will outline later in this chapter) and reveal many facets of her talent. Wagner-Martin (2004) believes that these stories show Kingsolver as a novice writer, in fact. One connection that is perfect for the classroom, however, is tied to the beginnings Kingsolver crafts in her short stories, particularly when placed beside the opening sentences of her essays as a lesson in beginnings for young readers and writers. Her "opening sentences . . . both grab the reader's attention and lead the reader to a conclusion that fulfills the promise of the opening," as Francine Prose taught Kingsolver (Wagner-Martin, 2004, pp. 68–69). This same concept can be found in the work of Edgar Allan Poe, as I will discuss in Chapter Two. "Rose-Johnny" deals with Native-American characters and shows Kingsolver coming to terms with themes associated with multicultural tensions. Drawn from her work in journalism (discussed below), "Why I am a Danger to the Public" stands as a vivid example of the use of detail and precision in fictional writing. Wagner-Martin (2004) identifies "Extinctions" and "Quality Time" as two of the better stories in the collection, tying Kingsolver's fiction to her own growing concern for family.

ENTRY POINT

Whether introducing students to the short stories of Kingsolver or the genre in general, Kingsolver's essay from *Small Wonder,* "What Good Is a Story¿" raises questions about why short stories are often ignored in modern America and about what the nature of truth is. This essay can establish a sense of discovery and skepticism in students as they consider or reconsider the value in short stories—in contrast to simply analyzing short stories in the textbook because the teacher asks them to write an essay. The essay also serves as an invitation, ending with "Good fictional tales will always be my pleasure, my companionship, my salvation. I hope they're also yours" (p. 214)

Poetry from Kingsolver comes to the reader in one collection as well, *Another America/Otra America* (1992); while Kingsolver refrains from calling herself a poet, her collection of poetry is difficult to ignore. Published in both English and Spanish, the collection makes a strong political statement in the content of the poems and the bilingual presentation. Chapter Six offers a number of ways to include the poems of Kingsolver in our classes during the study of poetry, as a connection with nonfiction, as an avenue to addressing multiculturalism, and as a tool in our need to address the increasingly complex issues raised in America concerning native and non-native speakers of English.

Less acknowledged than even her volume of poetry is Kingsolver's first nonfiction book, *Holding the Line.* This book captures, however, much of the writer and person Kingsolver became from the time she walked away from academia until the time she became famous as the writer of *Poisonwood Bible.* In the early 1980s, Kingsolver worked as a journalist covering the strike of the Phelps Dodge copper mine. This work reveals her concern for the little person, the average workers, those who find themselves at disadvantages they did not create. Wagner-Martin (2004) notes that Kingsolver approached the writing of this book-length journalism with an eye on *character*—oddly in contrast to the thematic nature of her novels (p. 57). Kingsolver eventually fictionalizes the people involved in the strike in *Animal Dreams,* as noted earlier, but this book concerns us as teachers primarily in the formative impact it had on Kingsolver the woman and the writer.

Kingsolver's best hidden treasure, however, is her two collections of essays—*High Tide in Tucson* (1995) and *Small Wonder* (2002). Both collections will be the primary focus of Chapter Two, but I want to offer a few introductory comments here as well. *High Tide in Tucson* reveals the person Barbara Kingsolver in a direct way that her fiction avoids. There is a voice of a living, breathing, struggling human in her essays—a voice that is direct, confrontational, humorous, and enlightening. The essays are engaging. They are filled with the people, the politics, and the events of her life, but they go beyond those details in ways that draw in readers and students for opportunities to learn indirectly and directly. Essays deal with her daughter's hermit crab ("High Tide in Tucson"), the impact of a librarian on her life ("How Dewey Decimal Saved My Life"), conflicting views of child rearing ("Somebody's Baby"), Kingsolver's continuing love for playing music ("Confessions of a Reluctant Rock Goddess"), and facing the power of American missiles ("In the Belly of the Beast"), among many other topics typical and atypical to all her works. These essays display beautiful craft, but they also provoke as most of her work does.

While *High Tide in Tucson* seems inspired by Kingsolver's own life, *Small Wonder* opens with clear seed of purpose: "I began this book, without exactly knowing I was doing so, on September 12, 2001" (p. xiii). Alluding to Adrienne Rich, Kingsolver announces that *Small Wonder* collected essays often forced the reader along with Kingsolver to dive in the wreck that is America and America's involvement in the post-9/11 world. In this collection, we see Kingsolver's tendency to confront at its fever pitch. While many of the essays are political overall, several pieces weave the political with a wide range of topics—the importance of place ("Knowing Our Place"), her daughter's love for a pet chicken ("Lily's Chicken"), the horror that is TV ("The One-Eyed Monster, and Why I Don't Let Him In"), being a mother and being a daughter ("Letter to a Daughter at Thirteen" and "Letter to My Mother"), the value in short stories ("What Good Is a Story¿"), confronting sex in writing ("Taming the Beast with Two Backs"), and a consideration of poetry ("Stealing Apples"). Some of the essays are cowritten with her husband, but all of the essays represent the mature voice and stance of Barbara Kingsolver as a concerned human being and as a gifted writer.

While I have attempted here to offer a brief but comprehensive introduction to the published writings of Kingsolver, I also hope that I have established the wealth of literature that she offers our classrooms, both in craft and in topics. Now, I will turn to the thematic range of her writing, a quality that raises her work above many writers and speaks to us as readers, students, and teachers.

Confronting the Politics of Theme

DeMarr (1999) describes Kingsolver as "person of strong convictions which she is unafraid to voice and to live by, convictions which suffuse both her writings and her private life" (p. 1). As a writer whose work we are bringing into the classroom, I can add that Kingsolver is a writer of conviction who rises above mere statement to stories and writing that *speaks*. From her essays and poetry to her wonderfully crafted fiction, Kingsolver approaches a number of thematic topics and motifs that are rich issues for students to wrestle with as growing readers and writers. Let's look at some of those areas broadly here for further background.

Cultural and Racial Divisions

Kingsolver's works more often than not address the concerns and conflicts that arise from differing cultures as they clash. Her works are notable for addressing Mexican-American concerns (*Animal Dreams*), Native-American concerns (*The Bean Trees, Animal Dreams, Pigs in Heaven*), Guatemala refugees in America (*The Bean Trees*), civil unrest in Nicaragua (*Animal Dreams*), and Belgian colonialism in the Congo (*The Poisonwood Bible*). As noted earlier, Kingsolver (1995) is drawn to the "places where disparate points of view rub together—the spaces between" (p. 154), and for her, those spaces often involve the conflict that comes from cultures that rub together. Her works address these tensions at both the more general surface levels and at much more personal and less easily defined levels. We can also bring Kingsolver into our classes as an example of complex explorations of culture and race, as a contrast to the dangers of oversimplifying and trivializing these issues by removing the people from the discussion and touching on the ideas alone. Students, for example, become engaged with the people of her novels first, then they move to the abstractions such as "race" or "culture" or "oppression." The degrees of empathy and genuine emotional response are some of the most significant qualities Kingsolver's writing bring to academic settings.

Socioeconomic Inequities

"But popularity in the economically stratified school went hand in hand with wealth, and the popular kids were the children of merchants and attorneys," explains Wagner-Martin (2004, p. 14) in her biography of Kingsolver. From childhood, Kingsolver appears to have developed a highly sensitive perception of socioeconomic imbalances, fueled throughout her young life by her own experiences, first, with her father's work as a doctor and then in highly impoverished areas of the world. That conscience, personified by Hallie in *Animal Dreams,* fills many of the events and the characters of Kingsolver's fiction. Later in this book, we will look at helping students develop a sociological (or Marxist) lens for viewing literary topics; Kingsolver's works are ideal for discussing the forces that create socioeconomic levels in America and throughout the world. Poverty is not something to be taken lightly or ignored, Kingsolver reminds Americans throughout her works—even when our own lives in a prosperous country seem blessed with plenty. Confronting wealth and poverty is a dominant theme running through all genres of Kingsolver's writing that stirs both the casual reader and the student. Kingsolver stands as a uniquely American writer who places social justice about material success.

Nature and Ecology

In *Prodigal Summer,* Deanna struggles with how she feels about snakes and coyotes; in *Animal Dreams,* Grace organizes the women of her hometown to fight for the very life of their water. While Kingsolver has a clear message that cherishes nature much like Thoreau and a clear political stance that promotes an ecological view of the planet, her works confront students with the complexity of these issues as humans constantly struggle with our drive to industrialize and invent even as it conflicts with our need to protect the very planet we hope to improve. Her explorations of nature and ecology overlap with her own ongoing arguments about science. Science as a field has the conflicting qualities of contributing to industrialization and mechanization while also valuing the natural world. Kingsolver offers a continuous voice against the worst of American industrialization, and she stresses the promise that nature holds for humanity. As David King Dunaway explains, "[c]onnectedness is . . . an outgrowth of Kingsolver's life-long study of ecology, in which she was trained in college and graduate school"—situating her concern for nature and ecology within other thematic concerns such as family, culture, community, and alienation (Wagner-Martin, 2004, p. xiii).

Alienation

While many of Kingsolver's concerns are clearly topics of the adult world, she deals wonderfully with a topic close to all adolescents—alienation; "Kingsolver's theme of seeing herself as some kind of misfit runs throughout many of her essays and interviews," notes Wagner-Martin (2004, p. 11). Often intertwined with her concern for ethnicity and socioeconomic distinctions, Kingsolver develops characters who find themselves outside of a community or culture. The quest for belonging is strong in her work, and it resonates well with teens and young adults. While alienation themes often address our alienation from other humans, Kingsolver also explores humanity's alienation from nature and from our emotional and spiritual selves. The broad range of alienation themes makes Kingsolver's works effective in our English classes, but she avoids some of the nihilistic characteristics found in other works dealing with this theme. Although realistic in style, Kingsolver's works resonate with an essential optimism that celebrates humanity and human nature while warning us of our potential for darker outcomes (other modern American women, such as Alice Walker, share this quality with Kingsolver).

Political Activism

A woman of conviction, Kingsolver is also a woman of action who imbues her works with characters often defined by the actions they take as well as the actions they avoid. Her characters often personify the theory that belief must be an action. The Stitch and Bitch Club of *Animal Dreams* reflects the power of collective activism, but her characters are often faced with decisions that call on them to act from a moral stance—such as the conflicting moral stances taken within the main conflict in *Pigs in Heaven* concerning the fate of Turtle. The dilemmas that drive the decisions are particularly interesting to students themselves, forming the beliefs that will drive their actions as adults. This thematic focus also manifests itself in her nonfiction and poetry with a similar power to her fiction. Most if not all of her writing is political activism in and of itself, along with the political activism it explores (such as Hallie in *Animal Dreams* or the refugees in *The Bean Trees*) and the political activism it inspires (notably her skeptical view of the current patriotism in America driven by our responses to September 11, 2001). Once readers and students are confronted by political activism by Kingsolver, their perceptions are at least changed—regardless of where anyone falls on a narrow political spectrum. Much as Margaret Atwood can be described in her work, Kingsolver is no ideologue, not easily discounted with political labels.

Issues of Marriage and Family

The public discussion about what counts as a family, what marriage means, and such is as vibrant today as ever. The very public and often divisive nature of those debates, however, may prove to be fruitless. Earlier, I noted that Kingsolver's fiction usually begins with and revolves around a question. Her works force students to reconsider their views of family (What constitutes a family?), of parenthood (What characterizes motherhood or fatherhood?), of the role of family members (What is a wife's duty to her husband? A child's to a parent?), and of the trauma of divorce (Can divorce be a good alternative?). While Kingsolver's fiction (such as the portrayal of the father in *The Poisonwood Bible*) or her essays ("Stone Soup," for example) often suggest or even directly state Kingsolver's answers to questions of marriage and family, the value in her writing is that it raises these questions for students to consider as readers and as writers themselves.

Feminism

The worlds of Barbara Kingsolver's writing are our own, but the voices of those stories, poems, and essays are primarily those of women. Like Margaret Atwood, Kingsolver does not simply parrot some stereotypical "women's agenda," as some often try to characterize the feminist perspective. What Kingsolver work offers is a view of *how* women often view this world and *how* the world often treats women—sometimes showing little differences between the genders, sometimes showing great contrasts. Wagner-Martin (2004) connects, again, this concern for feminism with her other thematic concerns and how these ideas were developed in Kingsolver's early life: In college, Kingsolver "[thought] of herself as a feminist, already impatient with the married women of her parents' generation for succumbing to the conventions of the good wife" (p. 33). Yet, such a powerful skepticism about the "conventions of the good wife" stands seamlessly beside Kingsolver's own unwavering commitment as a mother. Often integral to her feminist perspectives are explorations of how gender differences grow from cultural traditions or religious dogma; as well, Kingsolver looks closely at those gender differences as they play out in multicultural settings where characters from multiethnic backgrounds attempt to live in harmony. Ultimately, nothing is simple in her consideration of gender issues and gender roles, but she clearly confronts the claim that modern America is gender blind.

Community and Place

If we see Kingsolver as a political writer as she and most critics do, we must also see her as a writer whose work is firmly grounded in place, both in the sense of a tangible place (a specific town, such as Tucson) and in the sense of those qualities of *community* that create a place (a family, a club, an organized protest). Settings and the communities of those places are central to virtually everything she writes. Her fiction is vividly of *somewhere,* such as Taylor fleeing Kentucky and settling in Tucson or Deanna becoming so closely tied to Zebulon Mountain that she can barely have a life apart from it, but even her personal essays seem to grow from wherever Kingsolver is or has been at that time. She is a woman who literally *moved* outside of the United States to protest a war, we must remember.

ENTRY POINT

"I have places where all my stories begin," Kingsolver (2002) explains in the first sentence of her essay "Knowing Our Place," in *Small Wonder* (p. 31). This essay is a vivid discussion of the importance of the place of Kingsolver's composing and serves students well as an opening consideration of place as a thematic focus in all of her novels. Along with her consideration of place, Kingsolver also offers readers wonderfully crafted sentences filled with figurative language, distinct for their nonstandard surface features, and charged with apt and vivid verbs. This essay can serve as a lesson on craft, particularly as related to crafting nonfiction pieces (since we tend to emphasize craft primarily in fiction and poetry in the English classroom). Beyond using this essay as a discussion of essays as a genre, Kingsolver confronts the reader with fine distinctions—"food, like rain, is not a product but a process" (p. 39). Statements such as these fill Kingsolver's writing bringing a poetic quality to her prose. Students can begin with this kernel statement and pursue classroom discussion about "product" versus "process" as well as draft their own original writing; the statement from this essay might inspire students to write essays, a critical analysis, an argument, or even a poem. "Wildness puts us in our place," Kingsolver offers toward the end of her discussion of place, manipulating the meaning of the central term of the essay, "place" (p. 40). First, we can lead students to explore the beautiful complexity of English words (some dictionaries list 15 definitions of "place"), and then, we can allow students to wrestle with how nature does often put humans in their place—hurricanes, tsunamis, disease.

Colonialism

Most directly, *The Poisonwood Bible* explores colonialism with the Belgian involvement with the Congo (at the time of the novel), but throughout Kingsolver's work, the broad concept of powerful entities imposing themselves on less powerful people is dramatized. What right has one political power to control another community or culture or country? Or, whose perception of this world matters? Kingsolver helps the egocentric nature of all of us to reevaluate the nature of truth as we continually sift the universally true from the relatively true. Children often exist in a state of provincialism—the feeling that *their* perceptions and *their* experiences are typical and even *right* for everyone else. Literature is uniquely capable of broadening the perceptions of adolescents and young adults. Kingsolver's solid anticolonialism stance can serve as an excellent avenue for rattling students' cages, for pulling aside their blinders. In the early part of the twenty-first century, Americans are facing our impact on the rest of the world, brought about by the direct impact the rest of the world had on our soil. This sense of separateness conflicting with a reality of interconnectedness weaves its way through most of Kingsolver's works. While students may be drawn into the details of history found in *The Bean Trees* (searching the facts of Guatemalan history in the 1970s and 1980s) or *The Poisonwood Bible* (What did Belgian colonialism actually mean?), they soon come to see the parallels with the world they currently inhabit, whether it is Iran (direct military force) or Japan (American pop culture infusing a society). This theme, along with others, reveals why Kingsolver is a valuable source for integrating literature into courses other than English; students could begin a consideration of colonialism with America's genesis sprung from a revolt against colonialism, a revolt that some believed suggested an end to colonialism in the world.

Human Nature

I was disturbed the first time I came across a negative review of Alice Walker's *The Color Purple*. I found that a fairly wide range of critics found her so-called "happy ending" to be a flaw of her work. As I have explored the work of Kingsolver, I have discovered a similar refrain. Kingsolver happens to be an artist who holds a particularly optimistic view of human nature; Wagner-Martin (2004) notes that Kingsolver came to terms with her "eternal optimism" during the writing of her first novel, a perspective formulated while reading Flannery O'Connor (p. 61). That optimistic view stands in contrast to the often dark view common among the literary and the pessimistic view held by Christianity (notably the varying degrees of emphasis placed on Original Sin). Most teens I have taught find the discussion of human's basic nature fascinating—especially when they are confronted with optimistic opinions such as those held by Emerson and Thoreau or by modern novelists such as Walker and Kingsolver.

Contrasting Belief Systems

Not separate from other thematic topics found in Kingsolver but integral to many of them is her concern for the conflict that arises when belief systems collide. It may be characters with different views of a woman's place, or it may be two lovers with conflicting ideas about happiness or commitment. But found in nearly all of her fiction is the direct conflict of *belief,* the struggle of one mythological system against another. *The Poisonwood Bible* approaches this topic dramatically with the Price family failing to conquer an African belief system with a fundamentalist Christianity; then we see issues of belief blendings and assimilations concerning Native-American cultures or a variety of cultures from Spanish-speaking countries. While we would be doing Kingsolver and her works a disservice to reduce her message to endorsing "good" belief systems over "bad" ones, we can argue for students that the conflict created by systems of belief is worth our consideration without our prejudices, without our assumptions that can leave us blind. The complexity of separating right from wrong is possibly best captured in *Pigs in Heaven,* where Kingsolver portrays conflicting views as essentially equally justified in the characters of Taylor and Annawake Fourkiller (who are both driven to do what is best for a child).

Language

If writers naturally feel drawn to the power of language, then we can certainly claim that *political* writers are doubly caught in the gravitational pull of language—language that expresses, language that empowers, and language that imprisons. In English classes, we have a profound responsibility to share this concern for the power of language with our students, particularly as members of a free society, as members of a democracy. Kingsolver's characters—such as Reverend Price in *The Poisonwood Bible* or Grace as a teacher in *Animal Dreams*—often personify the power of language (both for good and for harm), and Kingsolver herself shows the power of language through her own writing—the craft of expression in the many genres of her work. In our English course, we can use Kingsolver's works for her own craft of language and for the literary motifs that run through her fiction, her poetry, and her essays.

As Wagner-Martin (2004) states, "most of Kingsolver's later novels . . . are driven by theme, by the ideas she wants to be sure to express" (p. 57). Themes are the big ideas that can serve learning well. We can bring Kingsolver to our courses because she doesn't preach themes; she confronts themes. As well, her confrontations are wonderfully crafted, providing English teachers with to address students as readers *and* students as writers.

Confronting the Politics of Craft

Many forms of art are engaging, and many writers might prove to be highly readable or eagerly read by high school and college English students; those facts alone do not make a writer's work appropriate for our classrooms. In the current climate of high accountability, we need to be sure that we are able to change what we teach and the way that we teach it for the benefit of our students and ourselves. The themes or topics of writing are key for exposing students to ideas, but without craft that writing is inadequate for academic study or for writing models. Kingsolver is a writer who engages the reader with her topics, with her stories, and with her craft. Her writing is serious business.

As I will explore more fully in the following chapters, the *how* of Kingsolver's work is ideal for the English classroom. As with her thematic tendencies, Kingsolver's works, in all genres, offer a rich source of technique and purpose. The following devices and references are common in her works, thus serving as rich ground for critical analysis and for modeling the best of writing:

- *Animal and nature imagery.* Her thematic concerns for nature and ecology are often expressed in her use of imagery and motifs connected with the animal and natural worlds. The Deanna sections of *Prodigal Summer* are titled "Predator," and *Animal Dreams* and *Pigs in Heaven* reveal the animal motifs in their titles. Kingsolver's use of imagery often rises to the level of motifs; this unifying structure of technique helps students see how purposeful *writing* contributes to meaning. Kingsolver's use of animal and nature imagery certainly connects with those themes, but the use of imagery and of motifs can be explored as they contribute to meaning. Far too often, we have students identify techniques for the sake of identifying techniques; our broader goal should be to help students connect technique (purposefulness) with meaning.
- *Setting.* As noted in the discussion of theme, the place of Kingsolver's works is often as central as the characters or narrations themselves. A sense of place is emphasized in her nonfiction as well as her fiction. I will discuss the use of Kingsolver's nonfiction in Chapter Two, but I would emphasize here that Kingsolver's works help show students that writing craft is found in the best writing of *all* genres. Often students come to believe that craft is found only in fiction and poetry and certainly has no place in the writing of students. We can explore place in the writing of Kingsolver to move students beyond "setting is the where and when of a story" to a consideration of how place (both the physical setting of when and where along with the abstractions—such as emotional connections tied to the physical place—that give a place its character) works within a larger purpose. Kingsolver's concern for place can be placed beside other writers who share this focus, such as William Faulkner (whose narrative technique in *As I Lay Dying* is mirrored in *The Poisonwood Bible*).

- *Vivid and rich diction.* Much of our work as ELA teachers involves words as we help foster our students as readers and writers. Kingsolver's rich diction and precise vocabulary (including her language drawn from the sciences) help as we create authentic lessons for students. About Deanna's father, the narrator in *Prodigal Summer* explains that he "didn't know the word *fledge,* but he knew what it meant" (p. 361). This is typical of the authentic concern for words that works its way through much of Kingsolver's works, a concern that young readers and writers need to develop. Here, the poetry of Kingsolver may serve as a starting point, although her nonfiction and fiction often exhibit rich language that is itself poetic.
- *Characterization.* Along with place, Kingsolver's work shines with character. The people of her fiction, as well as the people of her essays and her poetry, are fully drawn and engaging. The key quality of Kingsolver's characterizations is the complexity of the people; her worlds are populated with characters who struggle with right and wrong, who struggle with the frailties of being human. Many who teach the writing of fiction stress the importance of character, noting that fiction tends to emphasize characters and themes over plot (a distinction between serious and popular art that is worth considering with students). It is the people of Kingsolver's fiction, her poetry, and her essays who linger with readers and students.
- *Figurative language.* Young writers often struggle with strategies for giving their writing life and vibrancy. Metaphorical language gives writing life because it offers subtle and direct comparisons; meaning often grows from connections. When writing can connect, meaning often blossoms. Kingsolver has a masterful touch with metaphorical language—notably in her fiction and poetry but also distinctly in her essays. Her work reveals to students the craft of writing throughout genres. In her poem "Beating Time," Kingsolver laments the Arizona governor dropping poetry as a school requirement in 1997; for her, it is the power of language, not the pedestrian crunching of numbers, that matters, that causes children to "rise and dance to the iamb of the fans" (1. 25). The title essay of *Small Wonder* begins with Kingsolver hearing of an Iranian child being saved, adding that "the news of it came to me as a parable" and "I carried it like a treasure map" (p. 1). Whether in poetry, nonfiction, or a novel, Kingsolver enriches her ideas with figurative language that confronts readers and inspires young writers.
- *Detail.* In the beginning of *The Poisonwood Bible,* the reader watches as the Price family attempts to abandon those things they hope to carry to Africa. With meticulous details, Kingsolver reveals the

people and the messages of her works. Throughout the novel, the Price family's minds are filled with the products of America, the brand names of *things* that are uniquely American. We know Rachel from the details of her hair and her clothing (just as we know Adah from her linguistic peculiarities). Many student writers are inattentive to the details of their writing; it is difficult to see those things that we become so comfortable with that they seem to disappear. As well, young readers are often quite careless about noting details and the implications of those details. Kingsolver's essays and fiction are excellent fields of detail ready to be mined. It seems that this attention to detail in Kingsolver's writing comes from two sources—her scientific training and the lessons about writing she garnered from Francine Prose (Wagner-Martin, 2004).

- *Point of view, voice, narrator, speaker (persona).* From her own highly personal voice in her essays to the broad array of points of view in her novels, Kingsolver offers a wealth of variety concerning voice and narration in writing. As I noted in the discussion of themes, Kingsolver's works primarily reveal the voice of women. The richness of the feminist perspective is joined in her work by the richness of types of point of view. Her novels shift among versions of omniscient narrations, first-person narrations, and stream-of-consciousness narrations (particularly, the rotating points of view in *The Poisonwood Bible*). Again, Kingsolver offers students an opportunity to consider perspective, the nature of truth sifted through the viewpoint of those telling the stories.

• • •

This chapter has offered some broad background information about Kingsolver and her work to help teachers hoping to add her work or to expand the use of her work as part of the secondary or college English classroom. Essentially, I hope this introduction to Kingsolver and her writing has been an effective argument for adding her works to a curriculum. Additionally, I hope the use of Kingsolver will also lead to our reconsidering some of the things we do as English teachers (see the appendix). Chapter Two will now consider several ways to integrate Kingsolver's nonfiction into the reading and writing curriculum.

FOR FURTHER STUDY—BARBARA KINGSOLVER

Books

DeMarr, M. J. (1999). *Barbara Kingsolver: A critical companion.* Westport, CT: Greenwood Press.

This book-length critical discussion of Kingsolver offers a detailed discussion of her works through the late 1990s. For students and teachers, DeMarr's scholarship is extremely helpful for understanding the broad qualities of Kingsolver's writing.

Snodgrass, M. E. (2004). *Barbara Kingsolver: A literary companion.* Jefferson, NC: McFarland and Company, Inc, Publishers.

This "literary companion" is essential for the devoted Kingsolver reader, student, or teacher. Snodgrass includes a detailed chronology of Kingsolver's life and a genealogy before the primary section of the book, 122 encyclopedic entries covering Kingsolver's writing, themes, and a wide range of related information. For teachers planning to implement several works by Kingsolver as a regular part of your courses, a classroom copy of this book would be ideal.

Wagner-Martin, L. (2001). *Barbara Kingsolver's* The Poisonwood Bible*: A reader's guide.* New York: Continuum.

Wagner-Martin has prepared a brief book to aid readers and students of Kingsolver's most famous and most-often-assigned novel, *The Poisonwood Bible*. This is an invaluable tool for students studying the novel.

Wagner-Martin, L. (2004). *Great writers: Barbara Kingsolver.* Philadelphia: Chelsea House Publishers.

This newer work by Wagner-Martin is a literary biography targeted at student readers. The discussion is sophisticated, engaging, and insightful while maintaining a highly accessible quality. Students and teachers will find the book interesting and informative about Kingsolver as a person and her work.

Website

Barbara Kingsolver (Official Site) HarperCollins Publishers, 2003 http://www.kingsolver.com/home/index.asp.

This official website maintained by Kingsolver's publisher is an excellent and quick source of information on this author, including wonderful links within the site:

- "Kingsolver Bookshelf"—easy access to ordering all her books.
- "For Reading Groups"—discussion topics and questions for eight books (*Animal Dreams, The Bean Trees, High Tide in Tucson, Homeland and Other Stories, Pigs in Heaven, The Poisonwood Bible, Prodigal Summer, Small Wonder*).
- "Audio Library"—clips of excerpts from Kingsolver's books and easy access for ordering audio books.
- "About Barbara"—a brief biography, a chronology, a bibliography (the bibliography is thorough and excellent), and information on her Bellwether Prize.
- "F.A.Q."—just that, answers to frequently asked questions in Kingsolver's own words.
- "News"—the most current information about Kingsolver and her writing.

ENTRY POINTS AND CONNECTIONS

"Homeland" (*Homeland and Other Stories*), Barbara Kingsolver

"Flowers of Guatemala" (*Lifes Rich Pageant*), REM

"Cuyahoga" (*Lifes Rich Pageant*), REM

"Careful What You Let in the Door" (*High Tide In Tuscon*), Barbara Kingsolver

"Indian Boarding School: The Runaways," Louise Erdrich

"What Good Is a Story¿" (*Small Wonder*), Barbara Kingsolver

"Knowing Our Place" (*Small Wonder*), Barbara Kingsolver

Chapter Two

Confronting the Nonfiction Essay

David King Dunaway makes a strong assertion concerning Kingsolver: "It can be said of her what Jacques Barzun said of Aldous Huxley, that he was a good novelist but a great essayist" (Wagner-Martin, 2004, p. ix). And that is where we will begin as I discuss using Kingsolver in our English classes. As noted in Chapter One, Kingsolver has two engaging collections of nonfiction—*High Tide in Tucson: Essays from Now or Never* (1995) and *Small Wonder* (2002)—and her work offers English teachers a wonderful opportunity to address several nonfiction needs in our classrooms.

ENTRY POINTS

Both of Kingsolver's essay collections allow English teachers to begin the exploration of the essays through her references and allusions to two significant poems by women poets connected across the history of American poetry. At the end of "High Tide in Tucson," Kingsolver writes, "If the whole world of the living has to turn on the single point of remaining alive, that pointed endurance is the poetry of hope. The thing with feathers" (p. 16). Naturally, an excellent entry point to this essay is a mini-lesson on Emily Dickinson's "Hope is the thing with feathers" (1960, p. 116). A discussion of the craft in Dickinson's poem and of the theme of hope prepares students for Kingsolver's craft in her essay and her own thematic concerns with the contrast between "want" and "need" along with the human capacity for discrimination (the isolation of the individual is a theme often explored by Dickinson as well). *Small Wonder*'s "Foreword" opens with a direct reference to

Adrienne Rich's "Diving into the Wreck." Rich's suggestion of the greater "wreck"—in American society—establishes a critical view of America that is crucial for students to gain an awareness of before they are confronted by many of the essays in the collection.

"Write a nonfiction book, and be prepared for the legion of readers who are going to doubt your facts," warns Kingsolver (1995, p. 257). For our students, the reading and writing of nonfiction, of writing under the broad category "essay," present many problems as well. The concerns we can implement through the essays of Kingsolver include the following:

- Historically, the English curriculum has been disproportionately tilted toward the reading of fiction and poetry as well as writing analytical essays about that fiction and poetry. Drama also carries a much more significant part of our canon when compared to nonfiction.
- Nonfiction—occasionally called "informational text"—is far more common than fiction, poetry, and drama in the daily lives of adults—both as text they have to understand and as writing they are asked to compose.
- Nonfiction, especially in the form of personal essays, often springs from the lives of the writers; for emerging writers particularly, nonfiction writing can allow the students to focus more heavily on the *craft of writing* instead of generating content.
- The perception of "school writing" by both teachers and students can benefit from time to time by reexamining the assumptions of both teachers and students about essays. The published essays of a serious writer give teachers and students an opportunity to ground the broad conception of the form in authentic examples. I will also explore how teachers need to reconsider writing instructional and assessment practices, such as assigning writing and providing students with rubrics for guiding their writing and for assessing their writing.

STUDENT INSIGHT

When having students look closely at Kingsolver's essays—particularly her beginnings—students reveal some of the assumptions; in Ann Claire Felts' high school English class students made these comments about introductions in brief journals:

Throughout high school, my essays consisted of the same 3–5 sentence intro. The same intro which I knew everyone else in my class would have. However, reading outside of school challenged my perspective about introduct[ion] writing.

Camrey Ockowski

I was taught that the introduction [is] suppose[d] to support the title, but it starts talking about a crab. [referring to "High Tide in Tucson"]

Christopher Lindsay

We never really get to use our imagination or anything—like it has to be [written] the way they teach us.

Caitlin Rodgers

[Kingsolver's beginning] doesn't give you the simple predictable pattern; that's probably why it is entertaining.

Brandon Tripp

I was taught not to sound as though you're talking to someone. And I was told not to use contractions.

Jay Nesbitt

- On high stakes assessments of reading and writing at the state and national levels, students are asked to read and write essays, nonfiction (few standardized assessments of reading or writing deal with or allow fictional or poetic writing); the trend has increased from state assessments linked to accountability to the revised version of the SAT (2005). Even though we should reject much of the high-stakes testing mania for its inauthentic nature and its negative impact on students and their learning (particularly in reading and writing), we cannot ignore the fact of that testing and the ways in which writing is assessed on those tests. The assessment of reading and writing in standardized forms deals almost exclusively with informational text and with students composing nonfiction essays.

In this chapter, I will discuss the following lessons and strategies using essays from Kingsolver's two collections as starting points for the English classroom in secondary school or college courses:

- I often ask students to examine closely essay *beginnings* and essay *organization.* For the teacher and the student, these reconsiderations can include looking again at the effectiveness of writing rubrics. This lesson is a primary confrontation that is needed in our English courses to dispel the traditional template approaches to teaching writing (Thomas, 2005). We will look at learning to write essays as a discovery of writing qualities instead of prescribing those characteristics for students.
- *Memoir writing* can be explored as a literary form and as a writing assignment with many of Kingsolver's pieces. The memoir allows students to evolve as writers while working from sources of content that they know well, their own lives.

- Additionally, students can read Kingsolver closely, implementing *reading like a writer,* in order to unlock the *craft* of essay writing as a strategy for improving the analysis of writing and as a source for improving their abilities as writers.
- Along with the craft shown in Kingsolver's nonfiction, her use of literary and rhetorical strategies, teachers can use her work as a model for *authentic lessons in surface features*—examining her syntax, diction, grammar, and mechanics as discovery lessons for how writers use the language instead of memorizing misleading rules of language out of context.
- Kingsolver also challenges students with her *vocabulary,* offering students and teachers another authentic context for learning that can replace "vocabulary lessons" that often remain isolated and ineffective.
- Exploring Kingsolver's essays can include students working with persuasive writing, critical analysis, and documentation, as well. Once again, I will look at how to use authentic and holistic avenues to dealing with some of the isolated issues that we traditionally approach in English classes.
- Like her novels, Kingsolver's nonfiction deals with big ideas, big questions—often of a broadly political nature. Her work challenges students with complex explorations of *themes* that are both engaging and powerful. We will examine many of the themes acknowledged in Chapter One.

While using Kingsolver's essays as part of our literature curriculum is important, the essays also can serve as vital sources for our writing curriculum; let's look at the essays in order to confront the essay as a form first.

The Essay—Confronting the Form to Discover the Form

Kingsolver's two collections, *High Tide in Tucson* and *Small Wonder,* include a key though easily missed addition to their titles—the simple word "essays." As evolving readers and writers, students are constantly defining and redefining genres to sharpen their ability to comprehend and to express. Sophisticated readers identify genre or writing form as a frame of reference when reading; we *expect* an Op-Ed piece in the newspaper to do certain things by the nature of the form—offer an argument, reflect the voice of the writer. Sophisticated writers anticipate that readers follow that same strategy when they read, and those writers work in varying ways within those parameters for a form, sometimes conforming to them and sometimes leaping outside those boundaries.

The essays of Kingsolver provide several opportunities to rethink essays. Here, I will discuss activities that confront the following three areas:

- Essay beginnings are traditionally taught to student writers as comprising an *introduction,* which is often portrayed as a somewhat lifeless component that directly identifies a *topic* and *thesis.* Traditionally, we have defined this introduction as containing three to five sentences. When students read, however, essays by professional writers, they are exposed to quite a different concept of essay beginnings that refute the school "introduction," "thesis," and arbitrary guideline for the number of sentences.
- Essay form and development are often taught to student writers with the same template approach, which is contradicted again by professional models of essays.
- Providing students with rubrics to guide their essay writing and to assist teachers when grading often falls into the same template trap as the instructional situations discussed above. However, a scale drawn from the qualities demonstrated in one of Kingsolver's essays can help avoid those pitfalls (Figure 1). The ideal process for developing such a scale is to have the students themselves identify the qualities of a Kingsolver essay (or any essay by an established writer) and turn those qualities into guiding questions for their own writing. (The sample scale in Figure 1 is not intended, of course, to be a universal template, as I believe no such template exists.)

Figure 1: Kingsolver Scale

Note: I tend to use the 5–1 scale as equivalent to the traditional A, B, C,

Does the piece express a *moral conscience*?	5 4 3 2 1
Does the piece carry a strong *sense of place*?	5 4 3 2 1
Does the piece fulfill *coherence* and *unity of form* established for the reader?	5 4 3 2 1
Does the piece describe, inspire, or suggest *political action* for the reader?	5 4 3 2 1
Does the piece reflect the *craft* of writing?	5 4 3 2 1
Does the piece display a *command of language* by the writer?	5 4 3 2 1

D, F, but a rubric of characteristics can also be developed by the teacher with the students for each number depending on the needs of the course.

The larger instructional goal, here, for teaching the essays of Kingsolver is to support those of us who are looking to move our reading and writing instruction away from narrow practices to more authentic ones; that struggle has been central to me for all of my twenty-plus years of teaching at the secondary and college levels. The template approach to teaching the essay has two strong influences that we need to consider closely and ultimately set aside. First, teaching students to write essays within an artificial template springs from a misconception that novices *must* begin any new performance with rigid structure; learning theory and the evolving field of writing instruction have found this assumption to be false (Thomas, 2005). Second, a growing body of research is revealing that high-stakes assessment of writing is reducing writing instruction to template writing through the negative impact of sample essays (Hillocks, 2003) and poorly constructed and misapplied rubrics (Mabry, 1999). If we shift our instruction of essay reading and writing to authentic models such as the work of Kingsolver, our students will be more proficient readers and writers—even on tests that are less than ideal at the state or national levels.

Beginning Again for the First Time

Many of us who teach English have fretted over the tendency for students to begin their essays without focus. We are often also overwhelmed with the anemic beginnings in our students' compositions. As readers, however, we turn to the first page of a beloved writer and find, "June is the cruelest month in Tucson, especially when it lasts until the end of July" (Kingsolver, 1995, "Creation Stories," p. 17)—a first sentence charged with allusion and wit. If we allow ourselves as teachers to offer to our students the opportunity to rethink how effective writers begin their essays, we can address the need for students to begin their writing with focus and with life.

ENTRY POINTS

Wagner-Martin (2004) identifies Kingsolver's short story, "Covered Bridges," as an effective example of Kingsolver exemplifying a lesson she learned from Francine Prose about the first sentence of a short story (p. 69); that lesson taught by Prose is a classic premise of Edgar Allan Poe, often cited as a "father" of the American short story. Short fiction often begins with a sentence (or opening paragraph) that captures the reader's interest, establishes a central concern (an effect, a theme, a tension, etc.), and raises some tension in the reader that will be fulfilled in some way. Students often can see this as *readers* but fail to make that connection as writers. Starting a discussion of essay writing with a consideration of how Kingsolver's "Covered Bridges" fulfills these qualities of effective short story openings can be a solid platform for asking students to consider how they begin their own essays.

Taking the first sentence and eventually a first paragraph from several of Kingsolver's essays, we can offer students a discovery lesson in the many effective ways to begin the essay, emphasizing that the key elements of beginnings are *establishing focus* and *engaging the reader* (not conforming to a set number of sentences, not fashioning a fill-in-the-blank topic or thesis statement). These beginning sentences from both Kingsolver's books of essays are excellent for a mini-lesson on beginnings, offering to students a set of first sentences that they can mine for a variety of ways to fashion their own openings; the following sample listing of examples includes the opening sentence, the essay title, and the technique that characterizes the beginning craft:

- "June is the cruelest month in Tucson, especially when it lasts until the end of July" (Kingsolver, 1995, "Creation Stories," p. 17)—allusion, wit.
- "When I left downtown Tucson to make my home in the desert, I went, like Thoreau, 'to live deliberately'" (Kingsolver, 1995, "Making Peace," p. 23)—literary reference.
- "Maybe this has happened to you: You are curled up on the sofa, with an afghan maybe, and the person you love is there too" (Kingsolver, 1995, "Semper Fi," p. 66)—hypothetical "you" situation.
- "As I walked out of the street entrance to my newly rented apartment, a guy in maroon high-tops and a skateboard haircut approached, making kissing noises and saying, 'Hi, gorgeous'" (Kingsolver, 1995, "Somebody's Baby," p. 99)—narrative technique, purposeful misdirection. (Misdirection is also employed in her "Lily's Chickens" from *Small Wonder.)*
- "In the catalog of family values, where do we rank an occasion like this?" (Kingsolver, 1995, "Stone Soup," p. 135)—question.
- "The drive from Tucson to Phoenix is a trip through merciless desert, where tall saguaros throw up their arms in apparent surrender to the encroaching cotton fields" (Kingsolver, 1995, "The Spaces Between," p. 146)—figurative language (personification).
- "Once upon a time, a passing stranger sent me into exile" (Kingsolver, 1995, "Jabberwocky," p. 222)—manipulation of genre.
- "I have places where all my stories begin" (Kingsolver, 2002, "Knowing Our Place," p. 31)—one-sentence beginning paragraph. (Also employed in "Flying," in the same collection.)
- "'Nobody ever gets killed at our house,' begins a song by Charlie King . . ." (Kingsolver, 2002, "The One-Eyed Monster, and Why I

Don't Let Him In," p. 31)—opening with a song lyric.

- "My daughter came home from kindergarten and announced, 'Tomorrow we all have to wear red, white, and blue'" [followed by four paragraphs of dialogue between Kingsolver and her daughter] (Kingsolver, 2002, "Knowing Our Place," p. 31)—dialogue.

Examining a series of opening sentences to essays can provide many discussions concerning establishing focus for writing and establishing tone for a piece. Later, students can explore several beginning paragraphs to these essays before reading the complete essays to connect more fully how the craft and variety of the beginnings are effective in the context of the whole piece. From these reading activities, students write their own opening sentences and paragraphs; it is extremely important that students begin to see that the large concepts that characterize vivid openings are expected in *all* their writing—from formal academic writing to personal narratives to short fiction and even poetry.

STUDENT INSIGHT

In Ann Claire Felts' class, we combined a discussion of Edgar Allan Poe's guidelines for beginning a short story with a fresh look at beginnings to essays (both published works and those written by the students). (See the activities included at the end of the chapter.) Students find these discussions frustrating and enlightening. At first, they are highly resistant to questioning the templates they have been taught, but they soon see through such approaches into the varied and effective strategies that Kingsolver uses in a variety of essays. Some of their comments about Kingsolver's opening to "High Tide in Tucson" follow:

[Kingsolver] uses wit and personification. The thought of a hermit crab being basically like a runaway creates . . . an image of a crab maybe signifying a runaway person. Maybe an immigrant. She establishes a tone.

Katherine Pajon

I think the most important goal of a writer is the reader. To keep the reader interested. She's trying to make jokes about the crab to make it more interesting and fun.

Jennifer Gutierrez

The tone she is using is in a way an exaggeration; she starts out with a humorous introduction.

Caitlin Rodgers

She sets up a tone that makes the reader wonder. She simply speaks a short seven-word sentence that makes the reader want to know more.

Jennifer Becker

These comments show students gaining an awareness of the importance of tone and literary technique, supplanting their own concern for a thesis and having the correct number of sentences. This sort of discussion raises the sophistication of students as readers and writers. Further, these discussions are important for students of all ability levels and all levels of experiences as readers and writers. *Even the weakest and least experienced readers and writers can and should have these explorations.* Now let's look at a few sample beginnings by the same students:

Maybe a three-year-old trying to paint a German shepherd's nails wasn't such a good idea.

Jennifer Becker

If you want to be successful, you have to be an encyclopedia with eyes, watching all events very carefully.

Ashley Reid

If she never wanted one, why did she make those mistakes? Life began before she was ready. A few "I love you's" and a magical night in Caracas suddenly turned a life of two into a life of one and a half. A couple of weeks later it was dead.

Katherine Pajon

Once upon a time in a small, poor town, a lady named Cenaida gave birth to a little girl which she named Jennifer.

Jennifer Gutierrez

These sample openings capture many of the qualities the students discovered in Kingsolver's essays, moving their own writing beyond simple compliance with misleading guidelines of what essays must be (lifeless guidelines, in fact) to authentic expression that gave the students a sense of empowerment and pride in what they could write.

Discovering (Uncovering) the Essay

Often, the more we try to prescribe in order to provide novices with the basics, the more their performances disappoint us. To foster beautiful essays by our students, we have to move to authentic instruction grounded in authentic samples. After challenging students to rethink the beginnings to essays, and to all of their writing, we can turn to a closer analysis of a complete essay in order to see *what makes an essay an essay*—in conjunction with traditional literary analysis (that certainly has its place as well).

Student readings of "High Tide in Tucson" as a discovery lesson, both to support their growth as readers and as writers, revolve around students asking questions such as these:

- What topic or thematic concern does Kingsolver establish in the beginning? How does she accomplish that focus?
- What tone or tones does she manipulate throughout the piece? How do those tones impact the point of the essay?
- What techniques does she employ to maintain coherence, focus, and organization?
- What writer's crafts does she employ in her nonfiction writing? How do they impact her meaning?

A wide variety of questions similar to these work well, but the point here is that reading an essay to discover the nature of *essays* is somewhat different than reading that essay for literary analysis.

Further, this activity moves ultimately to students becoming essayists themselves. A dynamic way to move from exploring the essay to writing an original piece is to add a new approach to the rubric (see Figure 1). Designing a *conceptual* scale, such as the one offered above, based on the authentic attributes of the essay by Kingsolver helps avoid the trap of template essays; as well, it provides both students and teachers a more authentic lens through which to assess the writing. A conceptual scale driven by questions supports more authentic prewriting by students and helps reinforce the open-ended nature of effective essay qualities.

Here, I have planted a few key seeds concerning using the nonfiction of Kingsolver in our classrooms. First, we can use her essays to ask students to confront their perceptions of the essay and our own traditional approaches to having students write essays. Next, we can use Kingsolver's own craft to model for students how they can be effective writers themselves. Now let's turn to using Kingsolver's work as a model of memoir writing in our classrooms, an essay form that can bring life to our students and our students to their lives.

The Memoir—"The Truth about Who I Am"

The essay that reveals both one or more moments in the writer's life *and* ideas or questions the writer has concerning the world at large is a particularly relevant assignment for teenagers. Kingsolver's essays in both her nonfiction collections tend to be grounded in one or more moments of her life that she transforms through her writing. "I wonder how I can ever know the truth about who I am," she reveals in the opening essay of *High Tide in Tucson* (p. 14). She might just as well have added a concern for how she or any of us can know one's self and the big questions of life.

CONNECTION

Louise DeSalvo, in her memoir, *Vertigo,* has written about the healing power of writing about one's life with purpose and with meaning (Myers, 2004). It's an excellent idea to use excerpts from her memoir in conjunction with "High Tide in Tucson," or many of Kingsolver's other essays, as an exploration of personal narratives that go beyond detailing scenes from the writer's life. DeSalvo and Kingsolver discover meaning from writing about their lives; then they craft their own writing to express meaning for their readers. Memoir writing and reading memoirs provide students with rich experiences that exemplify discovering meaning through reading and writing. *The act of reading itself is an act of discovery; the act of writing itself is an act of discovery.* DeSalvo's memoir is also a rich source for us as teachers of English since her own life story is that of a woman who writes and teaches English. When we join our students in the exploration of memoir writing as readers and writers, we raise the level of the authentic English classroom significantly by our participation and our teaching as a student.

STUDENT INSIGHT

One of the most effective lessons that can be developed from "High Tide in Tuscon" is Kingsolver's ability to narrate a single scene from her life, and within that narration, she both brings the scene to life and uses the narration to make thematic points that move beyond her life. The scenes are excellent models for close reading and models for students' own memoirs. In Heather Loftis' class, students explored Kingsolver and wrote their own brief memoir vignettes; what these brief passages show is the ability of students to tell their own life stories while also moving beyond those stories in an attempt to look for meaning for themselves and their readers:

> Not only did I come away from my experience working with Boys and Girls Club knowing how to do the Harlem Shake and Heel Toe, I also got a new-found respect for those of a different race. No, I am not a perfect non-racist person, but I truly have a new outlook on discrimination. I got a different point of view from being on the receiving side of racial discrimination. What a complete role reversal,

for a little white girl to go into an all-black club and come out with the respect of her peers. Not only did I learn about bigotry; I also learned about myself and how I can be content alone.

Katie Arthur

At fifteen years of age, I was a rather slim and lanky kid. Standing 6'1" and one hundred and forty pounds, I was a runner. I had dreamed of becoming the next Mark McGuire and Michael Jordan, but I was destined to be Martin Tiller, the runner. . . . As Americans, we focus on becoming the best we possibly can, and not settling for anything less. Ralph Waldo Emerson, in his essay "Self-Reliance," states that "[a] man is relieved and gay when he has put his heart into his work and done his best, but what he has said or done otherwise, shall give him no peace." Emerson captures the true essence of accomplishing goals and becoming the best you can be. As American citizens of today's society, we push ourselves through pain, hoping to seek out redemption in the end.

Martin Tiller

Life is a privilege. I realize now that I need to live each individual day to the fullest because I never know if it will be my last. I think I will be content to be the tortoise in the race and slow my pace, allowing me to savor each moment of my life.

Kelly Ellis

As I was growing up I met many arrogant people that had the belief that since my mother was seventeen years old [when she had me] she wouldn't be a good mother. I believe that since my mother was a teenager when she had me that made her a better mother. I have had many discussions with my friends about how they have lied to their mothers so they could go to a party or go out with friends. This is where I am different than my friends.

Treva Camp

Students need direct instruction in making the larger connections that more sophisticated readers and writers make unconsciously. These student samples show that with that direct connection, with those discussions of Kingsolver's essays as samples of how student writing *can be,* students can move beyond writing to fulfill guidelines to writing as expression.

When students write for writing exercises, they need strategies, not templates (Thomas, 2005)—notably strategies that can be identified in Kingsolver's work. Some of those strategies can include the following:

- Ask students to focus on the smallest scene possible; many young writers try to describe or cover too much. Focus. When I confer with students on their drafts, I continually prod them to zoom in—narrow on a smaller thing and explode the details around that narrowing.
- During the drafting of the scene, writers should choose a few writing techniques to guide the revision stages. One is implementing figurative language through the use of metaphor, simile, and personification. Another is questioning throughout the draft the selection of verbs. A third might be an attention to detail. Kingsolver's essay offers many examples of these three areas as models for students writing their own scenes. Ultimately, no specific techniques matter more than any others do (although some argument can be made that some techniques are best because they are appropriate to the purpose); it's the *use of technique* that matters most for novice writers who have been writing without purposeful technique. We have to move young writers from writing that is mindless (often more to comply with guidelines than to express anything the students wish to share) to purposeful composition.
- Students must accept that drafting is an act of discovery. Kingsolver probably did not know what the scenes in her essay meant to her or could mean to her readers until *after* the drafting process. Too often, students feel they cannot begin an essay until they have a thesis in mind. A thematic focus for an essay will come after one or more drafts for the great majority of writers.
- Caution students that their memoir or personal narrative need not be as long as Kingsolver's; that's fine. In fact, according to the level or experience of the student, the memoir should be much shorter than "High Tide in Tuscon."

Giving students these or other strategies while they explore a specific type of essay is one part of a broader strategy to drive our teaching of writing. Students need authentic models of the writing they hope to compose, support as they discover the concepts that guide those authentic models, choice in the content of their essays, and enough time to draft their compositions as working writers do, discovering the meaning of their writing and the process of their writing *by writing*.

Confronting the Craft of Essay Writing

Much of the motivation for bringing Kingsolver's essays into the classroom revolves around having students rethink their conception of essay writing and acquire the skills of an effective writer. "High Tide in Tucson" includes a wealth of the techniques and devices that characterize wonderful writing regardless of the genre; in fact, if Kingsolver's essays are included along with her fiction and her poetry, students come to see that effective writing has many similarities across genres.

As a source for *reading like a writer* activities or for craft lessons, "High Tide in Tuscon" offers examples of the following:

- Sophisticated and vivid use of figurative language weaves throughout the essay, such as with the personification of the hermit crab as "an outlaw against nature" (p. 1). Similes and metaphors carry many of her key points, clarifying for students the effectiveness of figurative language in nonfiction writing.
- Kingsolver has a knack for a wide range of interesting allusions; in this essay, the swing from Cinderella references to more sophisticated allusions to the Bible, Emily Dickinson, and Thoreau ("Buster marched to his own drum," p. 5).
- A central motif to the essay, tides, is wrapped in irony; "[e]ven a desert has tides," she offers early in the essay (p. 6). While tone is always a challenge in instruction, we can raise students' awareness that *all* writing carries tone and that the tone of *all* writing should be a conscious effort of the writer (even when the composition is a formal essay on Hawthorne's *The Scarlet Letter*).

STUDENT INSIGHT

In Kim Long's eighth-grade English classroom (we cannot start too soon with authentic experiences for our students as readers and writers), she pulled a passage from "High Tide in Tucson" to allow her students to explore literary technique and personal narratives. Her experience shows how Kingsolver's work can contribute to younger students gaining a more authentic perception of both craft and the essay. When she asked them what they learned, some replied:

Rashad Gregory: You can introduce yourself without saying "Hi, my name is . . ." and use good details that support the main idea of your story.

Morgan Brooks: I learned to show, not tell.

Catherine Flood: That you can have flashbacks.

Shaelyn Hammond: From listening to the hermit crab example, I learned what similes and metaphors are.

Courtney Maher: How to use similes. I never really used them. I knew how to do them. I just never really liked them.

The pattern we can see is that these middle school students are beginning to use the terminology of craft and to make some evaluations of the *purpose* of literary technique as opposed to simply identifying technique in other people's writing.

Using a Kingsolver essay to unlock the craft of writing in nonfiction can be joined by moving the students into an *authentic exploration of surface features*—unlocking Kingsolver's writing to see her syntax, her grammar, her mechanics, and her usage. Reading like a writer to discover and push the boundaries of students' grasp of surface features helps avoid the often fruitless task of approaching surface features in isolated and "rules-based" ways. Two activities are effective for this type of reading-like-a-writer experience:

- Either pull a brief passage (a paragraph of several sentences) or allow students to choose a paragraph to use as a model for writing an original paragraph that mimics Kingsolver's style in surface features and craft *only*. Students supply the content but attempt to follow the syntactical and grammatical patterns of Kingsolver's passage. Students can turn these in or exchange with other students to consider the success of their exercises. If you provide a passage for students, attempt to select one that has sentence variety, unusual grammatical constructions, and notable nonstandard features (such as a sentence fragment or comma splice). The exercise shifts the burden of analyzing grammatical usage to the student and allows, again, the student to discover those patterns in surface features, thus empowering the student instead of imposing teacher-based rules onto the passive student.
- Offer a mini-lesson on surface features that explores specific examples of Kingsolver turning against what students often consider "rules." In "High Tide in Tuscon," she ends the essay with several sentence fragments, one of which helps emphasize her allusion to Dickinson—"The thing with feathers," standing alone as if it were a complete sentence (p. 16). Surface feature lessons from authentic sources can turn grammar instruction from imposing simplified rules to discussing purpose and control over the ever-shifting conventions of language.

An Essay Begins with a Single Word

Vocabulary instruction, like surface feature instruction, has suffered a long and troubling history in English classrooms. When vocabulary instruction is isolated, decontextualized, it is ineffective; in other words, it doesn't transfer into authentic reading and writing by students just as isolated grammar instruction fails to transfer to student writing.

Kingsolver's work offers an excellent avenue to move away from traditional approaches to vocabulary instruction involving vocabulary books and tests, and toward an emphasis on building the vocabulary base of students as readers and writers and creating a classroom focus on *diction.* Before looking at diction in Kingsolver's work, let's look at the characteristics of authentic word study as it contrasts with traditional approaches:

- Shift away from vocabulary books, exercises, and lists; move toward increasing students' experiences with rich language through reading and classroom discussions.
- Increase instruction and assessment of vocabulary through focusing on the words that students use in their original writing. If you choose to or are required to provide separate grades for vocabulary or even spelling, pull those grades from holistic assignments, such as their essays.
- Create an atmosphere in the classroom that focuses on diction, emphasizing choosing the best word for the context and tone of a piece of writing along with encouraging students to build their own vocabulary libraries by a variety of strategies that are best for particular students. Do not ignore the importance of classroom discussions, the importance of your use of language as a model for students.
- As an integral part of English class, incorporate reading-like-a-writer lessons that focus on the words writers use and why they use them.

Now, let's turn to Kingsolver's essay as a source of diction instruction. In the first two paragraphs of "High Tide in Tucson," Kingsolver (1995) uses "ordinances," "murexes," "whelks," and "refugee" (p. 1). Students can be invited to respond to those words for several reasons: Some may be new to the students ("whelks"); some may be used in unusual ways ("local animal ordinances"); some may be technical terminology from a particular field ("murex"), and all of them matter to the whole piece in some direct way. Once they are introduced to the significance diction plays in Kingsolver's essays, a number of lessons are effective, such as:

- Ask students to move from reading to writing through a close consideration of diction; several characteristics common to Kingsolver include scientific and natural terminology, precise and metaphorical verbs, tonally rich words, and detail-rich language. Four groups of students can take each situation noted above and attack "High Tide in Tucson" for a class discussion of diction. From that students write brief exercises that focus on having them choose two of the areas from Kingsolver to employ in their own writing.

- Ask students to create their own dictionaries. A fundamental flaw of schooling is our insistence that novices memorize information before we allow them authentic experiences; as adults, we find that we internalize and come to understand *as a result of* those authentic experiences, not *before* them. One type of student dictionary is one in which students gather words as they read and write—noting the source of the word, including a direct quote of that word in context, identifying the unique quality of that word (such as the four categories noted above). An entry could look like this:

  don—to put on clothing," from Kingsolver's "High Tide in Tucson," "When I was twenty-one, I donned the shell of a tiny yellow Renault and drove with all I owned from Kentucky to Tucson" (p. 6). Precise verb choice.

- The dictionary approach to vocabulary instruction allows diction instruction to be individualized and also allows students to learn words through use. When they are writing or reading they have the dictionary for reference. To allow the entries to be alphabetized, students can use index cards or simply type the entries into a word processor or spreadsheet; above all, students should make the dictionary their own.

As teachers of English, we all probably find words fascinating; using Kingsolver's essays as a vehicle for taking our students to that same realization can be effective for the student and the teacher.

Confronting Persuasion, Critical Analysis, and Documented Essays

Our English classes traditionally address certain types of writing by students; those writing assignments can be augmented through Kingsolver's essays. Let's look briefly at persuasive writing, critical analysis, and documented essays. Following this section, I will explore several specific essays by Kingsolver that can be the source of these lessons.

- *All writing is persuasive.* An effective argument I have been making for years is that *all* writing is persuasive; fiction writers are making the subtle argument that their creations are real. Every English course I have ever taught has required students to write at least one composition that focuses primarily on argument. Using Kingsolver as a starting point, ask students to explore a wide range of arguments—Martin Luther King, Jr.'s "Letter from Birmingham City Jail," Thoreau's and Emerson's essays, Op-Ed pieces by syndicated columnists, letters to the editor in the local newspaper. (See the discussion below concerning connections you can make while studying "Making Peace" and "The Spaces Between.") Then ask them to write a persuasive composition that springs from some framework other than the traditional school essay—narrative scenes, a letter response, journalism, satire.

- *Critical analysis also deserves reconsideration.* The close reading and written analysis of texts are valuable learning tools for English students—particularly when they continue their education at the college level. When we begin to reconsider writing in our classrooms, we must be careful not to throw out the baby with the bathwater. The analytical essay is our baby in English. An interesting writing assignment is to have students write a critical analysis on a Kingsolver essay that was not discussed in class after their close analysis of an essay as a whole-class activity, and then to add a twist—students must attack the traditional literary analysis essay form when they write their essays. First, this analysis of nonfiction will help expand their range of verbal dexterity (they receive ample opportunities to analyze fiction and poetry) and it taps into the adolescent and young adult desire to push boundaries.
- *Documenting issues that matter matters.* The research essay that requires formal documentation is also a valuable part of the English classroom. A major instructional goal should be an emphasis on acquiring a strong sense of documentation (not simply following the guidelines of MLA). Kingsolver's essays are highly issue oriented. Have students write documented essays that spring from a political issue that matters to them, that requires that they immerse themselves in the issue in many ways, and that results in a composition they want to share and share well with a broader community. Ideally, these essays should be written for an audience other than the teacher. The assignment may begin best when you ask students to search for that audience as part of their selecting a topic. Many of the essays discussed below would provide ample topics for such essays.

Confronting Themes in Nonfiction

A primary reason for increasing the reading and writing of nonfiction in the secondary classroom is to help students come to see that good writing has more qualities in common across the genres than differences. Often because of the template approach to assigning student essay writing, students tend to see nonfiction as thesis driven, instead of theme driven (though they sometimes reduce fiction and poetry *only* to theme at the expense of the work as a whole). Kingsolver's nonfiction is theme driven, often weaving into the stories of her life political and ethical concerns for her readers. Kingsolver often asks readers to confront fine distinctions between concepts (such as between "want" and "need") and to confront a wide range of topics Kingsolver holds dear in her work—feminism, patriotism, family, ownership/capitalism, raising children, TV, place, evolution/science, and the value of short stories.

"High Tide in Tucson," like many of her essays, eventually settles into a theme, often in the form of an implicit question; in this essay she leads her readers "to distinguish *want* from *need*" (p. 15). As readers, students need to explore how Kingsolver herself settles that tension in the essay. Further, reading this essay can prompt students to wrestle with the same tension or with some other tension of their choosing. Students can be asked to distinguish between "want" and "need" or some other pair of concepts that often rub together in their lives. Class discussions and student essays can spring from this topic and similar distinctions made by Kingsolver in her writing.

In her "Letter to a Daughter at Thirteen," Kingsolver (2002) offers the classroom an essay that directly appeals to the female students (who are far too often ignored by our literary selections) and explores Kingsolver's own personal journey to feminism. "Feminism" as a term has suffered some popular damage throughout the 1980s and 1990s, particularly from the Right. Students need to have open and thorough discussions of concepts such as feminism in the classroom in order to explore their own ignorances and assumptions without fear of unfair judgment. In the essay, Kingsolver refers to key figures in feminism, Betty Friedan and Gloria Steinem, providing background for placing feminism in historical perspective.

ENTRY POINT

"Letter to a Daughter at Thirteen" includes Kingsolver's confronting an American icon for girls, the Barbie doll: "I tried to explain how this doll was an awful role model" (p. 149). Her sermon fails, of course. Students can often have the opposite reaction just as Kingsolver's own daughter did. Marge Piercy's "Barbie doll" can create an opportunity to discuss the feminist perspective of Barbie doll images of women before students read Kingsolver's essay. As companion pieces, they can lead to lively discussions and interesting student essays.

Along with discussions and essays on feminism, "Letter to a Daughter at Thirteen" provides several opportunities to confront issues that fit well into the English curriculum of high school and college; some thematic topics include:

- The relationship between mother and daughter (or parent and child) is introduced in the essay's first sentences, in which Kingsolver admits that mothers "spy" (p. 144). Students often embrace considerations of where the lines of privacy are drawn between parents and children.
- Much of the essay is concerned with Kingsolver's own admissions of struggling with low self-esteem and concerns about her appearance. The essay can lead to students discussing and writing about physical expectations for females in America, about all young people's struggles with self-esteem, and about whether these issues impact males and females in disproportionate ways. These discussions can also lead to asking students to work through their own and society's perceptions of "beauty"—a theme attacked in Piercy's "Barbie doll."
- A favorite topic for debate among students is how much freedom and control adolescents and young adults need and deserve. Kingsolver's essay expresses well how difficult this issue is for the parent; students can write a response to this issue from their perspective.
- Although she touches on this subject only briefly, Kingsolver does address modern rap lyrics and their tendency to be violent and degrading to women—and the propensity of young women to embrace these songs without taking offense. This is a vital topic for young people to confront—although the topic is not as simple as we who find the lyrics intolerable may think. Eminem is cited directly by Kingsolver and serves as a perfect focus for this discussion since most young people find his lyrics "funny," while adults see his attitude as disturbing.

Kingsolver's *Small Wonder* is a collection of essays that often question America's patriotic fervor as possibly drifting into jingoism, into a blind nationalism that causes more harm than good in the United States and in the world. Even raising this possibility has generated some harsh responses for Kingsolver from fans who had loved *The Poisonwood Bible.* Two essays—"Stealing Apples" and "And Our Flag Was Still There"—can lead students to reconsidering patriotism, to reconsidering how they view America. "Stealing Apples" originally appeared as the introduction to Kingsolver's poetry collection, *Another America/Otra America* (which also confronts the idealistic view of all things American); however, she highlights her own discovery of the Sanctuary movement—"an underground railroad . . . [that] provide[d] safety for Latin American refugees" (p. 232)—in the essay, confessing her own loss of innocence. "And Our Flag Was Still There" confronts America's patriotic fervor after 9/11 much more directly than "Stealing Apples," weaving her own unorthodox patriotism out of a story of her daughter facing patriotic peer pressure in kindergarten.

CONNECTION

In "Amber (Get) Waves (Your) of (Plastic) Grain (Uncle Sam)," John Gardner (1994) begins his musing on the Bicentennial with a child-based narrative similar to Kingsolver's "And Our Flag Was Still There": "A month or so ago I had a relatively drunken conversation (I was drinking, not he) with an eleven-year-old about Patriotism" (p. 95). Gardner's essay forces the reader to reconsider the American Dream and the traditional idealistic view of the Founding Fathers. Students can place Kingsolver's concerns about America's newfound patriotism in context with Gardner's redefinition of the American Dream of thirty years ago. While Gardner redefines the American Dream, Kingsolver redefines patriotism—offering a platform for students to create their own definitions of both. Gardner and Kingsolver represent a motif running throughout American literature—*The Great Gatsby, Of Mice and Men*—challenging the promise of the American Dream for all.

Just as Kingsolver questions the pervasive definition of "patriotism," she confronts the single-minded attitude in contemporary America about "family": "I dare *anybody* to call this a broken home" (p. 125). "Stone Soup" is Kingsolver's very personal musing about divorce and the definition of a healthy family. This essay is charged with aggressive language, made vivid by Kingsolver's command of craft: "Like a cancer diagnosis, a dying marriage is a thing to fight, to deny, and finally, when there's no choice left, to dig in and survive" and "A nonfunctioning marriage is a slow asphyxiation" (p. 138). The essay is fertile ground for discussing the concept of "family" and the impact of divorce on all members of a family; further, Kingsolver slips some provocative facts into the discussion that can fuel discussion or writing by students, the percentage of American children in poverty (20 percent when the essay was writtten in the 1990s) and the higher rate of teenage pregnancy in 1957 than the 1990s.

If confronting patriotism and family values is not enough, Kingsolver turns her skepticism to possibly the greatest blind spots in the American mind, capitalism and ownership, in "Making Peace" and "The Spaces Between." In both essays, Kingsolver offers concepts that are highly foreign to American students—that wealth, ownership, and the capitalistic system of supply and demand may have flaws, may fail under a moral microscope. Either or both of these essays can lead to a number of lessons and activities connected with capitalism and ownership:

- Student knowledge of the capitalistic system is often inadequate; these essays can lead to students conducting research projects on capitalism, socialism, and communism. Further, these projects can help students understand how economic systems connect with democracy and totalitarianism (and other forms of government).
- Students can use Kingsolver's essays as a starting point for research on the concept of "ownership" in diverse societies throughout history. What cultures have focused on ownership? Were early Native-American cultures different from modern Americans in the perceptions of ownership?
- Friedrich Engels and Karl Marx are mentioned in "Making Peace." Students could research these men and their economic systems to confront their lack of knowledge and misconceptions about them; a valuable opening activity is to have students brainstorm what they know about Engels and Marx. Have they heard of *The Communist Manifesto*? Engels' *The Origins of the Family, Private Property, and the State*?
- Starting with Kingsolver's remark "What a relief, to relinquish ownership of unownable things," students could write about—and experiment with—relinquishing ownership of things in their lives or compose an argument about what things are ownable and what things are not.
- Two passages from "The Spaces Between" make for effective writing prompts as well: "[B]earing witness is not the same as possession" (p. 155) and "I could live without electricity if I had to, but not without stories" (p. 156). The second passage can be manipulated by the student, replacing "electricity" and "stories," to make the essay topic personal and then elaborating on that.

ENTRY POINT

Kingsolver's "Making Peace" begins with a reference to Thoreau's rationale for secluding himself at Walden Pond. The essay's opening reference and its discounting of "ownership"—"What a relief, to relinquish ownership of unownable things" (p. 33)—works well as a modern introduction to many of the same ideas addressed by Thoreau in *Walden*. Thoreau's arguments are similar to Kingsolver's, but students often find Thoreau too far removed from their contemporary world to be taken seriously. When Thoreau argues that two outfits are unnecessary, students find that concept bound by the mid-1800s, but Kingsolver raises similar arguments in the 1990s.

While I have had great success with nearly all of Kingsolver's essays at one point or another, let me conclude this chapter by mentioning six more of her essays and the topics they offer our classes:

- *Raising children*—"Somebody's Baby" explores the contrast between American attitudes toward raising children and children in general with other countries' attitudes.
- *TV*—Kingsolver confronts a sacred cow for most students, the TV, in her "The One-Eyed Monster, and Why I Don't Let Him In." This essay always stirs arguments from students, and I myself jotted arguments in the margins as I read it—one of the few Kingsolver essays on which I have done that.
- *Place*—"I have places where all my stories begin," offers Kingsolver in the opening line of "Knowing Our Place" (p. 31). This essay is a great focus for discussing the use of place in one's writing, the use of setting by writers, and the importance of *where* a writer composes in writing workshop.
- *Evolution and science*—Particularly for teachers but for students as well, Kingsolver's essays offer an interesting perspective on education—notably her concerns for science education and on perennial controversies such as the teaching of evolution (as it is popularly called). In "Setting Free the Crabs" and "A Fist in the Eye of God," Kingsolver forces the reader to reconsider the whole field of science, the nature of scientific research, evolution, the teaching of evolution in public schools, and the tensions between religion and science.

ENTRY POINT

"What Good Is a Story?" shares Kingsolver's own reasons for loving fiction and specifically the short story as a genre. This essay raises a question many students have, "Why bother reading short stories (or fiction at all)?" As an entry point to studying the short story genre, the essay can create a discussion that can guide the entire short story unit—What makes a short story, a short story? I use similar questions to guide other genre units—What makes poetry, poetry? What makes art, art?

Ultimately, I believe as a reader and a teacher that Kingsolver's essays need to become major parts of our literature study and our writing programs in high school and college English classes because of the high quality of her writing as an essayist and because of the issues and themes that she confronts with conviction. Since this chapter is certainly not exhaustive, I will end with a major assignment concept that works well when addressing nonfiction in both the literature and writing curriculums:

- Ask students to write a major original essay that incorporates the style and techniques they have become familiar with while reading Kingsolver with those of the traditional required writing that students produce in school. Students should write a nonfiction essay that uses narrative structures and techniques, that integrates purposeful craft (techniques such as figurative language), and that incorporates researched information to raise the essay topic from the personal to the wider community. This assignment allows students to choose their topic, requires them to practice authentic essay writing, and places research and documentation in an authentic setting (students should explore the distinction between the scholarly documentation that they need to do in school assignments and Kingsolver's own apparent lack of direct documentation in her personal essays).

High Tide in Tucson

"High Tide in Tucson"
"Creation Stories"
"Making Peace"
"In Case You Ever Want to Go Home Again"
"How Mr. Dewey Decimal Saved My Life"
"Life Without Go-Go Boots"
"The Household Zen"
"Semper Fi"
"The Muscle Mystique"
"Civil Disobedience at Breakfast"
"Somebody's Baby"
"Paradise Lost"
"Confessions of a Reluctant Rock Goddess"
"Stone Soup"
"The Spaces Between"
"Postcards from the Imaginary Mom"
"The Memory Place"
'The Vibrations of Djoogbe"
"Infernal Paradise"
"In the Belly of the Beast"
"Jabberwocky"
"The Forest in the Seeds"
"Careful What You Let in the Door"
"The Not-So-Deadly Sin"
"Reprise"

Small Wonder

"Small Wonder"
"Saying Grace"
"Knowing Our Place"
"The Patience of a Saint"
"Seeing Scarlet"
"Setting Free the Crabs"
"A Forest's Last Stand"
"Called Out"
"A Fist in the Eye of God"
"Lily's Chicken"
"The One-Eyed Monster, and Why I Don't Let Him In"
"Letter to My Daughter at Thirteen"
"Letter to My Mother"
"Going to Japan"
"Life Is Precious, or It's Not"
"Flying"
"Household Words"
"What Good Is a Story?"
"Marking a Passage"
"Taming the Beast with Two Backs"
"Stealing Apples"
"And Our Flag Was Still There"
"God's Wife's Measuring Spoons"

Entry Points and Connections

"Hope Is the Thing With Feathers," Emily Dickinson
"Diving into the Wreck," Adrienne Rich
"Covered Bridges," Barbara Kingsolver
The Philosophy of Composition, Edgar Allan Poe
Vertigo, Louise DeSalvo
"Barbie doll," Marge Piercy
"Amber (Get) Waves (Your) of (Plastic) Grain (Uncle Sam)," John Gardner
"Making Peace," Barbara Kingsolver
Walden, Henry David Thoreau
"What Good Is a Story?" Barbara Kingsolver

Student Activities—Beginnings

Begin the Begin

I. Edgar Allan Poe's *The Philosophy of Composition* (1850)

> "I prefer commencing with the consideration of an effect. Keeping originality always in view—for he is false to himself who ventures to dispense with so obvious and so easily attainable a source of interest—I say to myself, in the first place, 'Of the innumerable effects, or impressions, of which the heart, the intellect, or (more generally) the soul is susceptible, what one shall I, on the present occasion, select?' Having chosen a novel, first, and secondly a vivid effect, I consider whether it can be best wrought by incident or tone—whether by ordinary incidents and peculiar tone, or the converse, or by peculiarity both of incident and tone—afterward looking about me (or rather within) for such combinations of event, or tone, as shall best aid me in the construction of the effect."

II. Reconsidering Beginnings

Consider these beginnings from Kingsolver's nonfiction:

- "June is the cruelest month in Tucson, especially when it lasts until the end of July" (Kingsolver, 1995, "Creation Stories," p. 17)—**allusion, wit**.
- "When I left downtown Tucson to make my home in the desert, I went, like Thoreau, 'to live deliberately'" (Kingsolver, 1995, "Making Peace," p. 23)—**literary quote**.
- "Maybe this has happened to you: You are curled up on the sofa, with an afghan maybe, and the person you love is there too" (Kingsolver, 1995, "Semper Fi," p. 66)—**hypothetical "you" situation**.
- "As I walked out of the street entrance to my newly rented apartment, a guy in maroon high-tops and a skateboard haircut approached, making kissing noises and saying, 'Hi, gorgeous'" (Kingsolver, 1995, "Somebody's Baby," p. 99)—**narrative technique, purposeful misdirection**. (Misdirection is also employed in her "Lily's Chickens" from *Small Wonder*.)
- "In the catalog of family values, where do we rank an occasion like this?" (Kingsolver, 1995, "Stone Soup," p. 135)—**question**.
- "The drive from Tucson to Phoenix is a trip through merciless desert, where tall saguaros throw up their arms in apparent surrender to the encroaching cotton fields" (Kingsolver, 1995, "The Spaces Between," p. 146)—**figurative language (personification)**.

- "Once upon a time, a passing stranger sent me into exile" (Kingsolver, 1995, "Jabberwocky," p. 222)—**manipulation of genre**.
- "I have places where all my stories begin" (Kingsolver, 2002, "Knowing Our Place," p. 31)—**one-sentence beginning paragraph**. (Also employed in "Flying," in the same collection.)
- "'Nobody ever gets killed at our house,' begins a song by Charlie King . . ." (Kingsolver, 2002, "The One-Eyed Monster, and Why I Don't Let Him In," p. 31)—**opening with a song lyric**.
- "My daughter came home from kindergarten and announced, 'Tomorrow we all have to wear red, white, and blue'" [followed by four paragraphs of dialogue between Kingsolver and her daughter] (Kingsolver, 2002, "Knowing Our Place," p. 31)—**dialogue**.

III. Critiquing Beginnings

Read the opening paragraph (below) of Kingsolver's "High Tide in Tucson." What techniques does she incorporate? What does she establish in that opening—tone, topic, effect, etc.?

"A hermit crab lives in my house. Here in the desert he's hiding out from local animal ordinances, at minimum, and maybe even the international laws of native-species transport. For sure, he's an outlaw against nature. So be it." (p. 1)

IV. Challenging Our Assumptions

1) Does the above opening paragraph conform to what you have been taught about introduction? How or how not? Explain.
2) What is the most important goal of any writer? How does the beginning play a part in that role?

V. Writing New Beginnings

Either select an essay you have already written this year or start from scratch to write an opening paragraph of your own. What do you want to establish? Now incorporate some of the strategies explored above or try something entirely new.

Chapter Three

Confronting *The Bean Trees,* Confronting the Novel

Sometimes the narratives of life *do* seem stranger than fiction. In her biography of Kingsolver, Wagner-Martin (2004) explains that the genesis of *The Bean Trees* grew from her doctor's recommendation for her to confront her insomnia. Hiding in a closet led to Kingsolver's first novel, which may be the most accessible of her works for the classroom, particularly when teachers and students want to be engaged readers more than literary critics (although, as I will discuss, the novel is ripe for traditional critical approaches as well).

DeMarr (1999) has explained that Kingsolver's fiction tends to begin with a question; in *The Bean Trees,* "that question concern[s] the ways in which people help each other come through great difficulties" (p. 43). Placing a somewhat finer point on the focus of the novel, Wagner-Martin (2004) notes that "[o]ne of the themes . . . is that there is a danger in ostracizing people who form nontraditional families from those around them" (p. 64). As these broad characterizations show, the thematic concerns of *The Bean Trees* are highly relevant to the emerging beliefs and struggles that most high school and college students face; as well, the novel touches upon the simmering discomfort in America over concepts of family, home, and marriage that ranges from concerns about the growing divorce rate (thus single-parent homes) to the nontraditional families in minority communities to the increasingly mean-spirited debate over allowing homosexuals to marry or form civil unions.

This first novel by Kingsolver is an excellent addition to the high school or college literature canon, both as a class assignment and as outside reading for students. Here we will look at using *The Bean Trees* for several instructional purposes—to explore novel forms, to expand the literary lenses through which students read and analyze literature, to discuss the historical backgrounds of the novel, to highlight themes, and to analyze a writer's craft.

Exploring Novel Forms

We can approach class study of a novel either as an exploration of a *particular* novel or as one example of a *genre.* During my own evolution as a teacher of literature and as I have watched hundreds of other English teachers approach novel study in the classroom, I have come to believe that we are more likely to fail with a particular novel if we see that novel as the *goal* of instruction instead of exploring it as an *avenue* to some other goal that stands beyond the novel itself. If we undertake a study, for example, of *The Great Gatsby* in order to prepare students on a selected-response test on the novel or even the 1920s, we have reduced the study of literature to simply accumulating facts and details. When we place *The Great Gatsby* in students' hands in order for them to work through the narrative for what that story reveals to them about the nature of human existence—and *how* writers shape those ideas through narration, characterization, and craft—then the novel becomes a source of meaning instead of yet another task to perform at the request of a teacher.

I have also come to believe that we are not required to expose our students to any set list of great novels—although this has been the source of debate as long as we have formally studied literature. So as I discuss *The Bean Trees* and some of Kingsolver's other novels in this and the following chapters, I am suggesting that the strategies are highly transportable to all of her works and to works by the many other wonderful novelists that we can bring into our classes. Recommending the works of Kingsolver requires only one sentence: Her work stands as writing of the highest quality in both craft and message. *That* is the guideline I believe we should use when bringing literature and students together.

As noted in Chapter One, DeMarr (1999) characterizes Kingsolver as a writer of political novels, but she adds that *The Bean Trees* can also serve as an exploration of two novel forms that we traditionally include in our literature study—the picaresque novel and the *Bildungsroman.* Adding these lenses to the arsenal students have at their disposal can expand their abilities to explore literature on their own since Kingsolver's works both fulfill many of the traditional characteristics of novel forms and offer several qualities that refute those forms as well. Let's look at *The Bean Trees* as a political novel, a picaresque novel, and a *Bildungsroman.*

The Bean Trees can serve as an excellent introduction to the political nature of all of Kingsolver's works and the political qualities found in literature in general. As well, this novel can be used to expand students' awareness of the political nature of literature after you introduce Kingsolver's essays, connecting and contrasting how nonfiction and fiction express political ideas and political themes.

This first novel by Kingsolver stands as a vivid example of the broadest meaning of the term "political" as it deals with the interactions among people and communities—how compromises and conflicts work themselves out within power structures. *The Bean Trees* essentially focuses on such a broad political dynamic throughout the novel. Students can both explore how those issues develop within her novel and share their own political ideas through nonfiction and fictional writings. We rarely ask students to analyze the politics of text and offer far too few opportunities for them to write politically. This novel is ripe for those experiences.

The politics of family, the politics of friendship, and the politics of cultures are all dynamic elements of everyone's life and can serve as strong thematic platforms for students to discuss and write about how these forces work within the novel and how they work within the students' own lives and the lives of people around them. Let's look at one way to have students confront both the political nature of the novel and their lives along with how they write about literature:

- The traditional approaches to literary analysis, the writing of school essays on literature studied in class, have included having students restate the analysis carefully covered in class and tacitly *endorsed* by the teacher as the literary authority and the sole guardian of the grade for students and having students write that analysis within very prescriptive (and inauthentic) templates. Teachers will find that if we directly connect the analysis of literature with a student's own natural need and interest in self-inspection, the literary analysis and writing of students both develop dramatically. One assignment (though the elements I discuss here are easily manipulated) can grow from a political theme that is highly relevant for students: "[T]he concern for others that leads to the development of deep friendships may also lead to political concern and involvement in political causes" (DeMarr, 1999, p. 43). Instead of analyzing *The Bean Trees* for students only to have them restate that analysis for us, we can give them a platform—this novel explores the politics of friendships—and ask them to look critically at that thematic concern in order to write a critical analysis that leads to their exploration of the political nature of friendship in their own lives. This hybrid writing assignment (critical analysis and personal essay) underlines for the student the need for authenticity in literary analysis and writing about literature. This assignment also exemplifies what I call "tethered choice." While student growth in reading and writing is highly correlated with how much choice they have in those experiences, we as teachers have some responsibility to mandate portions of that learning. Ideally, students should read and write with complete choice, but that is rarely practical. The assignment above allows students to choose which friendships in the novel they explore; it moves the responsibility of that analysis to the students (instead of the teacher transmitting it to the student) and invites students to explore the nature of friendship in their own lives. The choice is "tethered" since students have some power over what they explore and say, but the assignment does provide instructional parameters, ones that I feel are far more authentic and challenging than traditional guidelines.

While Kingsolver exhibits a strong sense of the political nature of human interactions at the most intimate levels, direct political issues are also raised in this novel through the subplot concerning Estevan and Esperanza—Guatemalan refugees who introduce the issues surrounding the U.S. government's involvement in Central America during the 1970s and 1980s. DeMarr (1999) focuses on the powerful characterization of Estevan and Esperanza that grows out of actual political unrest within Guatemala and between the United States and Guatemala: "Their political activity in Guatemala, which has led to their becoming refugees . . . is evidence of their bravery and integrity" (p. 53). Although studying this novel should lead to students themselves researching the political dynamics within Guatemala and between that country and the United States, teachers should also be aware of the violence and unrest that characterized Guatemalan politics and life throughout the 1970s, leading to the United States pulling out its military aid in 1977.

ENTRY POINTS

Composed in the mid-1980s, close to the writing of Kingsolver's first novel, REM's song, "The Flowers of Guatemala," from their album *Lifes Rich Pageant* is an excellent entry point for the novel since the song deals with the political issues of Central America and introduces students to the night-blooming flower, the amanita, which is paralleled in the novel by the night-blooming cereus. The novel and the song share political concerns and imagery, making the song appropriate background concerning Guatemala. The song can introduce both the politics of Guatemala in the 1970s and 1980s as well as establish the natural imagery in the song and the novel, leading to discussions of how imagery contributes to motifs and meanings in literature.

Fiction allows students to explore historical and political dynamics through how those policies and political perspectives look in the lives of people. Central American politics in the 1980s probably is now fairly vague to many adults; for high school and college students today, it is completely unknown. Students can begin with the novel and then research the history behind Estevan and Esperanza, bringing the world and literature together in the classroom.

STUDENT INSIGHT

During a class unit on *The Bean Trees,* Renee Lane had her students complete journal entries about dealing with refugees and America's responsibilities for such people. One student shows a great deal of compassion and sophistication in the following entry:

I believe [the U.S.] has a responsibility to help these people [refugees]. Americans started out wanting freedom and safety from Europe. We can't build our foundation on that and then turn people away when they need help like our founders did. We shouldn't sit by knowing these people need [help] and we have the means to help them and just [do] not simply because we find it an inconvenience.

Brittany Woodall

Another student mixes a concern for our involvement with Iraq with an interest in Mattie's illegal but moral acts of helping refugees:

I think the U.S. should provide financial support during social and political turmoil in other countries because I think if we support them with [the] military, then that could be a problem too. . . . In *The Bean Trees,* Mattie is giving, not just Esperanza and Estevan, [but other] immigrants financial support even thought what she did is illegal.

Mark Deichman

The historical issues surrounding Guatemalan refugees and those Americans like Mattie who risked breaking the law in order to fulfill their moral obligations seem to resonate with students. Some of these issues of a political nature trigger students' own *moral* concerns as we see in the journal entries above. Making those connections—among politics, law, and morality—can move the studying of the novel beyond the world of the novel, as I have mentioned above.

CONNECTIONS

Study of *The Bean Trees* can effectively follow a nonfiction unit on civil disobedience and political activism or lead into such a unit. In my high school classes and in freshmen English courses, a highly engaging and successful unit has been working through the concept of civil disobedience with Henry David Thoreau's "Civil Disobedience," plus Martin Luther King, Jr.'s "Letter from Birmingham City Jail" and the 1982 movie biography of Mahandas K. Gandhi, *Gandhi.* Students can begin to connect Mattie's political activism and personal risk within the context of several examples of people finding the need to place moral causes above government-enforced law. Two essay assignments often grew from this unit for my classes. One asks students to write some sort of argumentative essay, drawing on Thoreau and King as models for writing persuasive essays; another asks students to explore some personal episode of making moral decisions that seem to work against those forces requiring them to behave in some way that they find morally wrong.

Particularly in the context of the novel and combined with the nonfiction and film connections suggested above, students are being exposed to the importance of language within all political dynamics, whether it is among friends or among nations. Estevan and Esperanza along with many of the other characters in this novel and other novels by Kingsolver offer possibly the ideal political issues that must be explored in high school and college English courses—the political issue of language and the power of language. The novel offers students the opportunity to discuss how language connects and separates us—Estevan and Esperanza actually are separated by their native tongues but united through Spanish (DeMarr, 1999, p. 62)—and how Standard English matters—and doesn't matter—in the reality of living (Taylor reflects the nonstandard dialect of Kingsolver's Appalachian roots). The politics of community in a wide range of forms is observed time and again in this novel—raising issues of power, issues of culture, issues of language, and issues of race. Students can come to see that these issues are not issues just in novels or history but are components of their daily lives.

ENTRY POINT/ CONNECTION

For students, the classic authors and works can be uninteresting initially since the language and history often feel distant and cryptic.

Kingsolver's works can be linked through politics to many classic works, notably to a school favorite, Charles Dickens, a writer with a sharp social conscience. Dickens can become more vibrant for modern teens when they approach his works as social and political commentary. Like Kingsolver, Dickens was often countercultural, a writer who challenged the status quo. Literature that challenges the establishment makes a natural companion to the immerging recalcitrance found in teenagers. While Kingsolver's social conscience in *The Bean Trees,* such as raising issues about child abuse (DeMarr, 1999, p. 58), has social critics such as Dickens to thank for establishing a rich history of art as political activism, students may need an entry point into the work of Dickens. John Irving, whose novels are highly successful in high school and college English courses, offers a wonderful pair of entry points into Dickens in *Trying to Save Piggy Snead* (1996). In his essay, "The King of the Novel," Irving confesses that *Great Expectations* "is the novel that made me want to be a novelist" (p. 347). This essay clearly establishes Dickens as a political writer, a morally driven social critic, a tradition fulfilled by Kingsolver.

Studying the political novel is rare in American English courses, but one of the many responsibilities of English teachers in high school and college is to introduce our students to the entire range of literary study, including the specific novel types. DeMarr (1999) notes that *The Bean Trees* falls within the traditional parameters of the picaresque novel and the *Bildungsroman.* The traditional qualities of novel forms can provide a framework for analyzing literature and can provide a basis for considering how and why writers often manipulate those characteristics. Let's look at these two novel forms briefly here as a way to integrate Kingsolver into the more traditional English curriculum.

The picaresque novel involves a central character who is a rogue and satirizes society and includes a number of journeys. *The Bean Trees* conforms to these requirements well but also moves beyond them. The central character exhibits rogue qualities but is female rather than, as traditional, male. The satirical nature of the novel and the various journeys encountered by Taylor make this novel, in some ways, highly traditional. Students could explore the traditional characteristics of the picaresque novel and offer explanations of how *The Bean Trees* conforms to those characteristics and how it does not. Ultimately, they should begin to discuss how novel forms contribute to reader understanding, possibly asking them to look at the conventions of TV sit-coms, for example, as a parallel to novel forms in their daily lives.

CONNECTION

Just as Kingsolver's novel might be easily paired with Dickens, the picaresque nature of *The Bean Trees* can be paired with another major work in the traditional canon, Mark Twain's *The Adventures of Huckleberry Finn.* Kingsolver's novel is an excellent in-class study that can be expanded to students reading and discovering *Huck Finn* on their own. Once they have the frame provided by exploring the picaresque novel, they can look for those qualities in Twain's work. Again, with Twain's work, students see the social criticism embedded in characterization, Pap's abuse of Huck paralleling the horrific and abusive past of Turtle, and in the story.

As DeMarr (1999) notes, *The Bean Trees* fits into the tradition of the novel of maturation, the *Bildungsroman,* as well. Again, these novels tend to be male centered, such as James Joyce's *The Portrait of the Artist as a Young Man,* but a growing canon of novels dealing with female maturation exists as well and deserves to join the canon of works studied in our classes (consider Zora Neale Hurston's *Their Eyes Were Watching God*). When I discuss analytical lenses in the next section, you can see how feminist perspectives help expand the traditional approaches to literature; feminist criticism has begun to reshape the way that we discuss novels of maturation. Kingsolver's first novel demonstrates the more complex exploration of maturity that is typical of female-centered novels.

The Bean Trees certainly deserves classroom study on its own merits as a novel, but as I have explored above, the novel can serve us and our students well as a means of confronting the frameworks within which the novel often unfolds. Discussing the political nature of the novel may be an unfamiliar process for many of us, but looking at Kingsolver's first novel as a picaresque novel or a *Bildungsroman* fits well into the curriculum with which we are comfortable. Now let's look at expanding our comfort zones, and the consciousness of our students, a bit further by expanding the analytical lenses of students as readers and literary critics.

Expanding Analytical Lenses

Understanding novel types helps make students more sophisticated readers. In addition, increasing the number of analytical lenses students have at their disposal creates a certain sophistication, both for students as readers and as writers. Asking students of all ages to critically analyze literature is challenging, but even in the earliest grades, we can begin to build into the frameworks of readers lenses through which to begin to understand text. Kingsolver's highly political writing is also richly crafted, so her work suits well the traditional grounding of literary analysis found in most high school and some college classrooms, New Criticism (of the Brooks and Warren tradition). Most young students can appreciate the relatively objective and systematic approaches of New Criticism, which asks readers to explore how craft creates meaning. For example, a prompt grounded in New Criticism theory would ask students to consider how a writer's use of figurative language and tone contributes to the central theme of the work.

However, we have come to see that literature has many qualities that are beyond the scope of objective criticism. Kingsolver is typical of modern fiction in that she is often best analyzed with a number of critical lenses, notably feminist and Marxist perspectives (Wagner-Martin, 2004). As I mentioned before, even entry-level criticism is challenging for young readers; adding more sophisticated lenses can ask a great deal of high school and college English students. If we are to ask a student to view *The Bean Trees* through feminist and Marxist lenses, they need an introduction to those lenses with text that is less challenging than the novel. The following activity with a children's picture book can serve as an introduction to different analytical approaches as well as sharpen the traditional approach to literary analysis found in New Criticism.

ENTRY POINT

Doreen Cronin (writer) and Betsy Lewin (artist) offer the children's book, *Click, Clack, Moo: Cows that Type,* which can be read very quickly to a class and then discussed from both a feminist and Marxist perspective to introduce students to those critical stances. This children's story includes many of the motifs and themes found in Kingsolver's work—language, political activism, community, etc. *Click, Clack, Moo* develops a story about a farm where the cows begin to type notes to the farmer, demanding electric blankets. Eventually the hens are pulled into a strike that involves the cows and hens withholding milk and eggs until they receive blankets. Toward the end, a duck mediates the strike, and the cows and hens exchange the typewriter for the blankets—a classic compromise. The story ends with the ducks holding onto the typewriter and demanding a diving board for their pond. Characteristic feminist and Marxist themes run through this children's story. The power of language (the typewriter) and the power of work stoppage are typical Marxist issues, ones found in Kingsolver. The patriarchal head of the farm in conflict with the female workers, cows and hens, provides a basis for feminist considerations as well. This children's story also includes craft in the form of onomatopoeia, dialogue, characterization, and motifs, and so it can lend itself to New Criticism so students can compare and contrast various analytical strategies.

STUDENT INSIGHT

In Renee Lane's tenth grade class, she introduced Marxist and feminist criticism through *Click, Clack, Moo* as a way to explore many of the themes of *The Bean Trees*. In several writing-to-learn activities, students showed sensitivity and sophistication in their understanding of the novel and Kingsolver's themes, commentary that appears to have grown from expanding their analytical lenses to include feminist and Marxist perspectives. The following journal entry is typical:

The violence in this novel comes [in many different forms]. For example, Turtle was apparently abuse[d] by her previous "caretakers" because she had many bruises on her when Taylor went to the Broken Arrow and was going to wash and dress her. Lou Ann was also a victim of violence; she was beaten by her father, brought to the attention of the reader when she saw the belt she had long ago been hit with. Another example of violence in the novel is the illegal aliens were killed. . . . The significance of the different forms of violence referred to in the novel is that no matter what your background or origin, you are always subject to violence. There are things in life that no one can escape.

Ross Hanna

Lane's tenth grade English class also listened to the REM song, "The Flowers of Guatemala," as a way to discuss both the night-blooming flower motif and the social conflicts in Guatemala in the 1980s. One activity asked students to explore poetic language and prose along with voice by having students paraphrase the song lyrics into an original paragraph. One sample paraphrasing of the song shows a great deal of sensitivity for the context of the lyrics and the tone of the speaker:

When I came here I had my doubts, but as I looked around I observed the kind and gentle people. They are friendly and content. As I looked deeper I realized that there was something strange happening. The flowers were growing at night. A specific flower. It grows everywhere and on everything. The type of flower is called the "aminita"; it is extremely hard to miss once you realize its awkward beauty. At day, they just close up and ignore the sun, because as soon it senses it, it will close up as if it were sentenced to solitary confinement. They cover everything!

Todd Warlick

Once we have raised students' awareness of the political nature of Kingsolver's writing and expanded their analytical lenses, we need to place students in new situations to see them apply those lessons beyond the classroom discussions. Kingsolver's "Homeland," the title story of her only short story collection, can provide teachers with an opportunity to assess students without reducing *The Bean Trees* to a selected-response test or to the traditional critical essay assignment, where students simply restate all that has been explored in class. The story can serve as the text for a writing assignment. I often do not ask students to write an analysis of a work already discussed in class (such a practice can encourage students to merely repeat what has been discussed instead of generating meaning for themselves), but I will ask them to write a critical analysis of a similar work. For example, after reading *The Scarlet Letter*, I have students write a critical analysis on "The Minister's Black Veil." After reading *The Bean Trees* and discussing the work in class, students can try out their new critical skills on a brief but similar piece such as "Homeland," a new text that has many of the same qualities that they have explored in the novel.

Confronting Historical Contexts

Lindquist (2004) promotes the use of historical fiction in the teaching of social studies because it can create interest; it can provide content knowledge many students lack; it offers a richer picture of history; it places historical facts in context; it highlights "the complexity of issues"; it expands the perspectives through which history is viewed; and it helps to integrate the academic disciplines. For our purposes here, I would add that we, as high school and college English teachers, need to emphasize the history that is inherent in literature. Kingsolver's work often pulls the political from the historical—often fairly obscure historical events as far as the popular American consciousness is concerned.

In *The Bean Trees,* as I have mentioned, Kingsolver puts faces on the U.S. government's involvement in Central American affairs during the Reagan administration and the lingering impact of Native Americans being displaced by U.S. policies. Kingsolver's including Guatemalan refugees and characters with links to the Trail of Tears provides opportunities for students to explore those events *and* analyze how the historical events translate into literary and political commentary in fiction. This two-tiered goal can be assigned in a number of ways, all of which focus around these two broad approaches:

- Gardner (1999) argues that the goal of content teachers is to have students practice the content field as professionals do. In English courses, we often have our students practice literary analysis; additionally, we can ask our students to work and write as professionals do in many fields, notably historians. Either in groups or individually, students should work as historians to uncover the details and people involved in Central American political issues during the 1970s and 1980s and the events surrounding the Trail of Tears. The Internet provides a wonderful basis for students to research as historians do, to practice scholarly documentation for authentic purposes, and to evaluate their sources (much of what they find on the Internet may be inadequate or inaccurate sources, for example). Since Kingsolver's novel itself reflects her political bias, students can begin to analyze the bias inherent in all text and information. Guiding questions for this type of historical search can be:

- What appear to be the key details of this historical event? (Students should be introduced to triangulation—a researcher's technique that searches for multiple sources of data in order to increase the truth of that data.)
- Who were and who are the groups or people most involved in this event and how do their perspectives vary?

Students end this research with a variety of performances that include presentations such as PowerPoint or other multimedia programs, but we should also ask students to write as a historian writes.

ENTRY POINT

If we are going to move students into areas where reading and writing are integral elements of the field, such as in history, we can also begin to expand their understanding of how fields remain vibrant through varying perspectives. Just as we often tend to portray literary criticism as monolithic (the supposed objectivity of New Criticism), we imply that history is an objective display of what has happened on this planet. Relevant in many ways to using Kingsolver in the classroom is the work of confrontation historian Howard Zinn (who had a small entry point into the popular consciousness through a brief reference by the Matt Damon character in *Good Will Hunting*). In Zinn's *A People's History of the United States,* he explores the traditional topics of U.S. history in survey course but offers a Marxist perspective through the eyes of what we might call "the little people," those without power and those who have lost in the struggle. His *Declarations of Independence* is rich with essays that would fit in classroom discussions of U.S. involvement in other countries, particularly with our military actions such as in Iraq. This collection includes a discussion of just and unjust war that might fit well with the civil disobedience unit mentioned earlier as well.

CONNECTION

Along with introducing students to history they haven't encountered before, Kingsolver can be a link to writers students haven't encountered yet. The work of many Native-American writers has remained just outside the traditional canon of the high school English classroom. Although the work of N. Scott Momaday has cracked the pages of many school texts, few students have read a complete novel of his. *The Way to Rainy Mountain* is a natural companion to students exploring the Native-American experience in the United States and is suitable for outside reading. If students read Momaday or other Native-American writers after exploring Zinn's perspective on history, they can begin to question who should tell any group's story. This sort of living debate within a field, history, allows students to see content areas as vibrant and evolving instead of fully formed as they appear in the pages of a textbook or on the information listed for them through the overhead.

- More directly connected to our goals in English is the fact that Kingsolver uses history in her fiction for political and *literary* purposes. In other words, how do historical events create meaning within the work? The Central American issues raised in the novel are personified by the characters Estevan and Esperanza, who offer opportunities to explore characterization and the language motif that runs through much of Kingsolver's work. The Trail of Tears lurks beneath the character of Taylor and her ancestry, and it supports the journey motif throughout the novel. Young readers and writers often feel they have completed a literary analysis by simply identifying technique. A student will make an observation such as "Kingsolver incorporates the Trail of Tears to support her journey motif in the novel." The next level, explaining *why* that technique matters both within the work and beyond the work, is more difficult for maturing readers and writers. In *The Bean Trees,* the use of historical events and political themes can support teaching students how *craft builds meaning.* Using this novel to help students sharpen their abilities to connect allows students to see the broader concept of making connections in all content areas and is directly useful in preparing students who are working toward either of the Advanced Placement courses or tests in English that stress, in the multiple-choice test and in the written assessments, a student's ability to connect literary craft with a writer's purpose.

The Bean Trees helps students see how fiction can broaden their understanding of history and of how historians work and think. It also serves well our continual need to stress to students that writers use their craft, their literary technique *with* purpose within the text and *for* purposes beyond the text.

Confronting Themes and Craft in the Novel

As English teachers, we *love* literature—and we *love* teaching literature; we love teaching literature in the ways that we were taught literature. Many of us often want to know how we can add literature to our classes, but we also want to know whether that literature can stand beside the classics and whether that literature can fit into the practices that make our field what we love to do—literary analysis, purposeful reading for meaning. The works of Kingsolver fulfill this need. Let's look here at the many thematic and craft elements that make *The Bean Trees* both a beautiful novel and a highly teachable work in our English classes.

Thematically, *The Bean Trees* establishes interests that have come to characterize Kingsolver the writer throughout her career. As mentioned earlier, much of her thematic concerns grow out of questions about those problems and ideas. These themes and motifs are central to the novel and can lead to a number of student activities—discussions, essays, research projects, etc.:

- Friendship, community, family, and motherhood are overlapping and interconnected thematic concerns that breath life into this novel. Kingsolver forces the reader to ask, What characterizes friendship? Community? Family? Motherhood? Often, as writers tend to do, Kingsolver dramatizes ideas in people and events that contradict traditional conceptions of those ideas—notably traditional definitions of "home" and "family" (Wagner-Martin, 2004, pp. 63–64). For example, throughout the novel, Kingsolver manipulates and dissects what makes motherhood *motherhood* through Mattie as a surrogate mother to Taylor, through the accidental motherhood of Taylor to Turtle, and through the motherhood of Lou Ann, Esperanza, and Taylor's own biological mother. Effective writing assignments from these thematic concerns can range from having students analyze how Kingsolver answers these questions within the novel to having students define these ideas themselves through a variety of genres; teens find defining "friendship" or "family" relevant and even cathartic in most circumstances.

STUDENT INSIGHT

While brainstorming for their essays on some of these themes, students in Lane's class wrote journal entries about both family and home.

The novel defines home in terms of people by the way Lou Ann and Taylor live. Taylor and Lou Ann are acting like a family and staying up half the night talking. In terms of geographical settings, the novel defines Taylor and her mother being in different states and still acting like a family.

Amy Harrolle

The two main characters in this novel are Taylor or "Missy" Greer and Lou Ann Ruiz. . . . These two characters show what the word "family" means even though it's not your typical idea of family—a mother, a father, and children living together.

Mark Deichman

The students in Lane's class found discussions of friendship, community, family, and motherhood engaging both within their analysis of the novel and in their own exploration of the concepts as connected with their lives as young people. These themes are some of the richest elements for students, and within those themes students seem to find the characters and situations about which they have the strongest feelings.

CONNECTION

Discussed in Chapter Two, "Stone Soup" (*High Tide in Tucson*) is an excellent essay that confronts issues of family and definitions of family (Wagner-Martin, 2004, pp. 63–64). If students have read the essay before *The Bean Trees,* they certainly could be asked to discuss the two works together. Or this essay could be included in the novel unit and used as a connection for students who wish to write on family or motherhood instead of on the novel directly. In the essay and in the novel, Kingsolver clearly wants the reader to rethink definitions of family and parenthood in order to move beyond the superficial characteristics and toward the essential qualities that create these relationships in healthy and productive ways. Kingsolver shows that Turtle may be better served in life with the strange family she inherits than with the mysteriously abusive people who abandoned her.

- Language and silence are powerful topics in this novel, and throughout Kingsolver's canon. What is the power of language and silence?,

Kingsolver asks; as well, she wonders, How does language unite us, and how does it separate us? I noted earlier that Estevan and Esperanza, though married and both Mayan, are separated by their dialects, thus forced to be united through Spanish. Ironically, Kingsolver's language motif is supported by a silence motif as well in the characters of Turtle and Esperanza. As students analyze Kingsolver's use of language and silence motifs within the novel, they can also be asked to consider the importance of talking and silence in their young lives and in their schooling. The way that talking and silence work within the authority structures faced by young adults is a powerful and valuable issue that can be broached through the characters in *The Bean Trees.*

- Kingsolver also wrestles with divisions—social, cultural, economic, gender, and religious. Marxist and feminist perspectives, explored earlier in this chapter, help students see the many forces that work within a society, forces that may not have clear sources or obvious intents. While we often can see that life isn't fair, we have a much more difficult time agreeing on why those inequities exist—or even how we can wipe away those barriers to equality. A novel allows students to explore these hard issues in a relatively more manageable setting.
- Activism, raising a political voice, is a natural extension of the division issues noted above. Kingsolver does suggest ways for the reader to address the hard issues of being human and of being an American, a steward of a free society. Mattie, who provides sanctuary for Guatemalan refugees, is the direct personification of activism in the novel, but Kingsolver's work carries throughout a message of acting on the world instead of being the victim of life. Layered with her message of activism, Kingsolver raises several political viewpoints—antiwar sentiments, concerns for nature and the ecological well-being of the planet, the horrors of child abuse (personified by Turtle), and serious reservations about the moral compass of government.
- A journey motif punctuates *The Bean Trees.* A classic motif of literature (often found in the picaresque novel and the *Bildungsroman*), the journey also supports a discussion of the novel as a work of maturation, as a work of discovery of self. As in many works of American literature, the initial movement westward by Taylor establishes a sense for students of how motifs and themes create meaning while connecting with larger associations within our culture. In other words, the journeys in the novel have *unique* significances that grow out of the novel itself, but they also depend on the reader having a cultural awareness of the westward move-

ment both in the history of America and its literature. The movement west has often been a journey of hope in our complex history, but that journey was often bittersweet—or simply a defining, though scarring, part of who a people have become. Students can begin to wrestle with the westward movement of America as it conflicts with the inconsistent history of American policies toward Native-Americans.

STUDENT INSIGHT

One student in Lane's class saw the forces behind the journeys characters take in the novel:

Taylor has been driven away from her home, but not because of her family, but for her sake. Taylor couldn't stand where she was living so she had to get out of there. Taylor's difference in moving away . . . [is she] leaves because she wants to, but everyone else is driven away by someone.

Kelliann Balon

Students can become highly sensitive to the complexities of how life develops; literature can provide an opportunity to move beyond simplistic explanations for why people behave as they do, why people leave one place called home to create a new place called home.

The beautiful part of teaching English revolves around the opportunities we have to discuss writing for its craft in lessons for our students. Simply put, serious writers do the things they do with *purpose.* In fact, purpose is what distinguishes the expert from the novice. Kingsolver demonstrates a full toolbox in her novel; *The Bean Trees* offers ample opportunities to explore the craft in fiction writing:

- Plot and subplot are often difficult elements for students. Kingsolver's novel relies heavily on character, but her plots and, notably, her subplots, provide enough support and twists to keep her characters vibrant. Although some critics take her to task for being overly optimistic, for having resolutions that are too neat or positive, Kingsolver weaves interesting and unique visions that are engaging, that support her drive to question, and that challenge the reader's preconceptions. The subplots of *The Bean Trees* may serve as a connection to more traditional works such as Shakespeare's plays.
- John Gardner, author of *Grendel* and a number of works on becoming a writer, often stresses that the lifeblood of fiction is characterization. In this first novel by Kingsolver, we see her interest lies

primarily with the people of her imaginary worlds. Yes, her political and thematic messages matter, but we can see that ideas concern her *only* in the context of how those ideas impact the lives of people—and for her as a writer, the lives of characters. A central lesson for us to emphasize to our English students is that *complexity* is a key to sophisticated writing. Kingsolver creates complex characters who wrestle with this world as we do.

- Kingsolver's use of narration is less well defined in *The Bean Trees,* but throughout her career, point of view and narration have grown to be key elements of her fiction. In her first novel, narration and point of view do offer an opportunity for students to explore purpose since the work shifts between first-person and third-person narration. For the novice writer, making unconscious shifts in narration, tone, or even verb tense can mar a work. For skilled writers, those shifts are purposeful—thus, effective.
- English students become adept at identifying the usual craft techniques such as metaphor, simile, and personification, but writers generally have a much broader arsenal. One technique that is often ignored is a writer's use of details—from the use of names to the precise description of how a character holds a pen to the use of product names, such as Campbell's soup. In this novel, names of characters support themes and questions raised by Kingsolver. For example, Taylor changes her name, and she names her found child Turtle instead of her rightful name, April. Esperanza's name means "hope," adding ambiguity to the subplot of her and Estevan's situation as refugees.
- Natural imagery blossoms throughout Kingsolver's works; she loves the natural world, and it cannot help growing throughout her writing; Wagner-Martin (2004) notes that Turtle's "vocabulary increase[es] vegetable by vegetable," for example (p. 62). In *The Bean Trees,* she incorporates flower imagery (the night-blooming cereus) along with many references to nature and animals in her metaphorical language. The natural imagery is raised to the level of motif throughout the narration; students can begin to appreciate the unifying quality that literary technique provides. Natural imagery can create a nature motif that gives structure to the novel.
- DeMarr (1999) emphasizes Kingsolver's political focus, but she also notes that a sense of place, of setting, is a dominant force in Kingsolver's fiction; in this novel, Kentucky (the East) represents her "limitations" (p. 54), and Tucson (the West) stands as her hope. Throughout the somewhat episodic nature of the book, each scene is dressed in a place that matters: the picnic scene and the Lake o'

the Cherokees scene are just two examples.

STUDENT INSIGHT

Whether looking at the novel in traditional or nontraditional ways, overwhelmingly, Lane's students enjoyed this novel; they felt engaged and were spurred to think deeply and complexly about many issues both in the novel and in their own worlds. Typical reactions to reading the novel are reflected in these journal entries (see the prompts included below before student responses).

Discussion and Journal Prompts

1) Have you had a positive or negative experience reading *The Bean Trees* by Barbara Kingsolver? Explain and offer specifics where possible.
2) Write a paragraph (several sentences) that expresses the situation, the attitude, and the themes in the lyrics of REM's "The Flowers of Guatemala." Write the paragraph in the first person, reflecting the voice of the speaker in the song's lyrics. Pay attention to your style as you draft.
3) Should the United States provide financial or military support during social and political turmoil in other countries? Explain.
4) What responsibility does the United States have for people fleeing civil unrest and oppression in other countries, people who wish to enter the country to find freedom and safety?
5) How do you feel about the U.S. involvement in Iraq? Has reading *The Bean Trees* impacted your ideas? Explain.
6) Write a prose or verse piece that uses an image or symbol (as in the song and the novel) that reflects your view of the U.S. involvement with Iraq.
7) Currently, the United States is facing serious issues about both legal and illegal immigration. What do you believe the country should do concerning both legal and illegal immigration? Why? What impact does the threat of terrorism have on your position?

I use[d] to not like reading but reading her book made me want to read more. Also, it has taught me to care about more things and that it is possible that you can live without your parents. There is a world out there, and when reading *The Bean Trees* it has taught me to go and explore. You never know when something will happen but sometimes you are just stuck with it.

Austyn Boyd

The Bean Trees was a very interesting and positive experience for me because it shows how a typical girl from Kentucky can go so far. It interested me that Taylor was so successful on her own. . . . She is a strong person in showing she can go this far on her own. This novel has a positive outlook on things and shows people a good way of life.

Ross Hanna

A further reflection of the power of this novel is the work produced by Lane's students in essays written after exploring *The Bean Trees.* Some of the passages from the students' essays follow:

Knowing about the wisteria plant, its required care, its twining vine, its rapid growth, and its ability to grow anywhere gives the reader insight into the characters of *The Bean Trees.* Taylor, Turtle, Mattie, Lou Ann, Esperanza, and Estevan are all interwoven together due to various circumstances. With each situation they become closer and closer and eventually become a family. There is a vine in all life that is thick, strong, and growing with a lot of people helping to make it grow. . . . By a twist of fate, Taylor finds hope in her journey through Mattie. Mattie acts as a mother for Taylor—the mother that Taylor left behind.

Mark Diechman

Taylor describes Oklahoma in a way that mirrors how the Cherokee Indians would have described the Trail of Tears when" . . . the sight of it filled me with despair. I had never imagined that any part of a round earth could be so flat."

Amy Harolle

Taylor's life is just like the wisteria vines. She had to grow and thrive at first without any help just like the vines in the desolate park. It is a miracle that either lived.

Cody Collins

Turtle put herself into a stage of muteness for a while, as if in solitary confinement, to punish herself for something. Until she found happiness in the form of Taylor. . . . Every character in the novel finds happiness, but the one character that stands out the most is Taylor, who also finds herself.

Todd Warlick

Before moving on, I want to share a comment from the teacher herself, Renee Lane, about her experiences in implementing many of the activities above. Her observation to me during her class's study of *The*

Bean Trees captures the cumulative effect that the novel clearly had on her class (one that moved many students to find other Kingsolver novels to read on their own). I share her email because many English teachers may read about adding feminist and Marxist analysis to English classes or introducing essentially political novels to the canon and believe that these might be overly ambitious efforts. Listen to Lane:

> We are doing the children's book today. I'm going to give them a chart to chart where they see basic Marxist and feminist characteristics in the children's book; then we are going to discuss where those same things show up in [the novel] and they are going to add that component. . . . They have already grasped the concepts of motifs and are ravenously identifying every motif every time it shows up in the book. I don't think they had ever heard the word before, and they think they have learned some new "make them look real smart" type of thing. They also loved Estevan's story about heaven and hell and the spoons. That really had an effect on them.

Lane's comment captures the essence of our need to expose *all* students to more than we traditionally attempt. It was clear to me and Lane that asking more of students as they read, discussed, and wrote about *The Bean Trees* was an empowering unit for the students—something we could imagine would please Kingsolver a great deal.

Confronting beyond *The Bean Trees—Pigs in Heaven*

"Since the 1988 publication of *The Bean Trees,* Kingsolver had been flooded with requests that she continue the story. Few characters had made such an impact on readers," explains Wagner-Martin (2004, p. 88). I can attest that as a reader myself I was drawn to Taylor and Turtle in a way that still causes me to miss them now that I have left the novels behind; as a teacher, I watched as students with excitement announced that they would buy and read *Pigs in Heaven* on their own.

The concept of sequels often elicits skepticism about the quality of the work—whether we are discussing movies or novels. *Pigs in Heaven* certainly refutes such concerns. The novel carries over from *The Bean Trees* the engaging characters of Taylor and Turtle, with their nontraditional family status and Taylor's personal struggles. Kingsolver creates from those characters a dynamic and believable conflict that centers around an even more complex twist in the relationship between Taylor and Turtle. After writing her first novel, Kingsolver discovered the 1978 Indian Child Welfare Act and followed a news story concerning the adoption of a Native-American child by a white family in Arizona (Wagner-Martin, 2004). Intrigued as she is by deep and complex questions, Kingsolver created the continuing story of Taylor and

Turtle, now threatened by a chance appearance on *The Oprah Winfrey Show* (Turtle saves a man's life and, as a result, receives media attention).

Pigs in Heaven explores the perplexing debate that rises from Annawake Fourkiller, a Native-American lawyer, seeing the talk show and eventually challenging the "adoption" of Turtle by Taylor. One of the most powerful aspects of the novel, particularly as a novel that is studied by high school and college students, is that Kingsolver creates sympathetic and persuasive characters in *both* Taylor (whom most readers already love) and Annawake (who could have easily been portrayed as the "villain"). While the plot itself carries interest and unexpected shifts, the real value in the novel is the rich characterization that drives the reader's own struggle to decide just what is best for Turtle.

ENTRY POINT

Just as Kingsolver herself was pulled into creating the conflict in *Pigs in Heaven* by her own discovery of issues within the Native-American culture, many students outside of Native-American communities have a poor understanding of those issues as well. While themes and motifs connected with Native-American history and mythology are often integrated in Kingsolver's works, this novel deals more directly with them. An activity that helps introduce students to Native-American motifs and themes is the song "Cuyahoga" by REM. The song explores the actual burning of the Cuyahoga River in Ohio that resulted from pollution; the historical events behind this song date from the mid- and late-1800s until the burning of the river reached national attention with an issue of *Time* in 1969 (a Web search will find a number of excellent sites that discuss the history and the legend of this burning river). The song opens the door to a discussion of issues of industrialization and progress, ecology and pollution, vivid diction and motifs, and the role of Native Americans in U.S. history.

Briefly, I will offer below some of the issues and assignments that can revolve around moving from *The Bean Trees* to *Pigs in Heaven*, either as an additional in-class assignment or as an independent extracurricular study:

- The novel can be the basis for students engaging in a debate or persuasive essay, taking sides in the conflict between Taylor and Annawake. This conflict can serve as an effective basis for asking students to argue through research. The 1978 Indian Child Welfare Act offers a starting point for the research concerning the legal issues surrounding Native-American children and adoption in general.

- DeMarr (1999) believes the novel "concerns the relationship between the individual and the community" (p. 94). Again, since Kingsolver tends to write fiction as the exploration of questions, students can be led to explore how both the individual and the community matter: What is the value of each and how does that value impact each as they overlap. One of the primary issues faced by students is balancing the tension between self and community, especially in our American democracy that values the individual so highly. DeMarr notes that the conflict is shown through Taylor as "individualism" and Annawake as "community values" (p. 99). Students can explore this larger theme beyond how Kingsolver personifies the problem in her narrative.
- Kingsolver's third novel fits well into our traditional approaches to literature, often the standards we are required to meet by accountability measures. As noted before, Kingsolver stands as a vibrant writer, one who exhibits the highest level of craft. This novel is suitable for literary analysis focusing on the following:
  - Novel structure based on three sections correlating to the seasons, spring, summer, and fall (DeMarr, 1999).
  - Narration contributes to the central conflict of the novel by revealing the story in omniscient point of view (DeMarr, 1999).
  - If students have read Piercy's "Barbie doll" (see uses of the poem in both Chapters Two and Six), they can focus on the character Barbie in this novel and how Kingsolver deals with issues of social pressures on women in America. With Barbie, Kingsolver confronts issues of fashion, eating disorders, and ultimately personal ethics as they reflect cultural ethics. While serious in intent, Kingsolver's characterization of Barbie is sharp satire worth exploring by students (DeMarr, 1999).
  - As with many of her other works, whether fiction, poetry, or nonfiction, this novel depends heavily on setting, a sense of place.

CONNECTIONS

As discussed in Chapter Two, Kingsolver often works through her own skepticism about issues such as patriotism and faith in the American dream. DeMarr (1999) sees Kevin, in *Pigs in Heaven,* as the personification of a naïve belief in equal access to wealth in modern America. This starting point can serve to connect students to classic American novels on the American dream—such as Fitzgerald's *The Great Gatsby* or Steinbeck's *Of Mice and Men*—but it also can connect students to a powerful nonfiction book on working in America at the poverty level, *Nickel and Dimed,* by Barbara Ehrenreich (2001). Ehrenreich's investigative and participatory journalism raises many questions about how much access low-income earners actually have to wealth or even the basic necessities in modern America. High school and college students find the work engaging and startling, a direct contrast to the attitude portrayed by Kevin in Kingsolver's novel.

- A lingering debate and problem faced by English teachers at the high school and college levels is how to address surface features (grammar, mechanics, and usage) effectively. Having students explore surface features in the context of literature is often highly effective in raising students' understanding of how surface features impact meaning and how surface features are purposefully incorporated by writers. The idiom and nonstandard grammar that run throughout the dialogue of the characters in *Pigs in Heaven* are ideal for such considerations by students. Looking at dialogue as a technique to develop characterization and having students write dialogue themselves allow students to work with surface features in authentic ways.

ENTRY POINT

As DeMarr (1999) points out in her analysis of *Pigs in Heaven,* much of the novel depends on contrasting mythologies in the American psyche and in Cherokee culture. The importance of understanding the nature of mythology and legend cannot be overstated for young students, particularly young literature students. One of the most effective and accessible discussion of mythology and legend is Joseph Campbell and Bill Moyers' *The Power of Myth,* which grew out of interviews with Campbell by Moyers (the work is also available in video format under the same title). Campbell provides students with sophisticated yet lucid explanations of the patterns in most myths and legends along with how myth matters in the daily life of humans. The novel works through many Cherokee legends as they intertwine with the struggle to determine who should be legally responsible for Turtle.

- *The Bean Trees* provokes classroom discussions of such novel types as the picaresque novel and the *Bildungsroman.* In addition, *Pigs in Heaven* continues Kingsolver's political nature as a novelist but also incorporates a manipulation of "the genre most deeply imbedded in women's fiction, the romance" (DeMarr, 1999, p. 114). Typically, novels do not conform neatly to any conventions of a genre form, especially literary novels (in the traditional sense of novels written with literary intentions such as high levels of craft and several layers of meaning). Students can use this novel to explore the conventions of a romance and how Kingsolver's manipulation of those conventions contributes to the themes she explores, notably those that deal with women and with relationships between men and women and between women and women (the power struggle between Taylor and Annawake, for example).

ENTRY POINT

We will again discuss the stories of Kate Chopin in Chapter Four with a discussion of *The Poisonwood Bible,* but it is appropriate to note here that Hinchey (Kincheloe, Steinberg, & Hinchey, 1999) identifies Chopin's "The Storm" as a highly provocative story that exposes students both to the manipulation of romance conventions and to satire, noting that students learn "about the difference between judging a story by established societal norms and thinking about an alternative value system a story may propose" (p. 143). Like Kingsolver, Hinchey wants to confront students who analyze literature through "autopilot evaluations" (p. 143). "The Storm" manipulates the language and plot of romance fiction; satirizes societal norms for women, fidelity, and marriage and challenges the reader as forcefully as Kingsolver does. The short story is quite brief, lending itself to a fairly quick introductory lesson.

• • •

Most readers and critics identify in Kingsolver's first three novels deep concerns for growth, captured in flowering and natural imagery. Her characters blossomed from page to page and even from novel to novel. This motif of her work appears vividly in her own life as a writer in the huge success of her next novel, *The Poisonwood Bible,* and the lush language and themes in the fifth novel, *Prodigal Summer,* which we will explore in Chapters Five and Six.

ENTRY POINTS AND CONNECTIONS

"The Flowers of Guatemala," REM
"Civil Disobedience," Henry David Thoreau
"Letter from Birmingham City Jail," Martin Luther King, Jr.
Gandhi (movie, 1982), Richard Attenborough, director
The novels of Charles Dickens
Trying to Save Piggy Snead, John Irving
The Adventures of Huckleberry Finn, Mark Twain
Click, Clack, Moo: Cows that Type, Doreen Cronin (writer) and Betsy Lewin (artist)
A People's History of the United States and *Declarations of Independence,* Howard Zinn

The Way to Rainy Mountain, N. Scott Momaday
"Stone Soup," Barbara Kingsolver
Pigs in Heaven, Barbara Kingsolver
"Cuyahoga," REM
The Great Gatsby, F. Scott Fitzgerald
Of Mice and Men, John Steinbeck
Nickel and Dimed, Barbara Ehrenreich
"The Storm," Kate Chopin

Chapter Four

Confronting *The Poisonwood Bible*

I have written this book specifically because I love the work of Barbara Kingsolver; the essays, poems, and novels have breathed life into my living as a reader, a student, and a teacher. Our English students need such experiences, often as a counterbalance to the many failed and incomplete experiences they have had with reading and literature in school.

As a single example of how a chance discovery can change a student and fill a teacher with happiness, consider Megan Alexander's exuberant email to me about one of her ninth graders:

> Guess what?! One of my girls discovered Barbara Kingsolver! She saw that I was reading *Poisonwood Bible,* and I happened to have another copy on my shelf, so she picked it up, asked me if it was a good book, and started reading. She comes in today and has already read 100 pages and she's just gushing over the language. This is a great book for her to read because it's about Baptist missionaries who go to Africa and try to "save" them, [and] a critique of such missions will be good for Paula. Help her consider different viewpoints. Ahhhh, these are the moments I live for.

Megan's enthusiasm as a young teacher and devoted reader of Kingsolver is possibly as exciting as the student's discovering a novel in her classroom, taking it home, and reading *by choice* over one hundred pages that same night. If we add to this scenario, Kingsolver's own impassioned words from the "Author's Note" at the beginning of *The Poisonwood Bible*—"I spent nearly thirty years waiting for the wisdom and maturity to write this book" (p. x)—we as teachers can see the tremendous potential this novel offers for our students.

When artists attain critical or popular success—or even both, as Kingsolver has—that artist can often identify one instance or work that stands as the point of his or her public recognition. For Kingsolver, *The Poisonwood Bible* is the work that has made her quite wealthy and highly regarded as a novelist and as a strong moral voice among contemporary artists. As well, Kingsolver is widely read outside of our classrooms at a time when many people fear that reading for pleasure is in an irreversible decline.

Confronting a Popular Novel—Teaching *The Poisonwood Bible*

While Kingsolver has not yet become a fixture among writers commonly studied in high school or college English courses, the popularity of *The Poisonwood Bible* has provided teachers with a wealth of materials to allow them to begin using this novel in classes. Literary criticism, biography, and study guides on Kingsolver are beginning to appear, most of which pay considerable attention to *Poisonwood.* This chapter will explore a number of opportunities for teaching this novel as an in-class or out-of-class project, but I will try not to overlap the large amount of resources and classroom ideas that already exist for this novel in contrast to the lack of such materials for her other works discussed in this book.

ENTRY POINTS

In the essay, "The Vibrations of Djoogbe" (*High Tide in Tucson*), and the short story, "Jump-Up Day" (*Homeland and Other Stories*), Kingsolver deals with African life (DeMarr, 1999, p. 119), making these works suitable entry points for *The Poisonwood Bible.* In "The Vibrations of Djoogbe," for example, Kingsolver herself discusses her own evolving awareness of and discoveries concerning Africa and its diverse culture, particularly when it seems foreign and disturbing to Americans. This essay, in typical Kingsolver fashion, revolves around overt questions raised in the discussion. Thus, the essay is an excellent entry point to asking students to research African culture and geography before attempting to grasp the vast amount of background information needed to fully experience the narrative of *Poisonwood,* as Kingsolver's narrative technique draws the reader inside each character and reveals the great world quite subtly. Because I have encouraged teachers to avoid direct assessments of literature that can be reduced to a cataloguing of details, "Jump-Up Day" can be paired with *Poisonwood* as an assessment tool by asking students to write about a passage from the story or the entire story. This parallel use of the story can be an entry point for the analysis of

Kingsolver's fiction or a summative assessment after students complete the novel.

Before turning to the novel directly, I want to identify several rich sources for teachers to use when teaching this novel. Both teachers and students will find Internet searches to be highly rewarding. The official Barbara Kingsolver website (www.kingsolver.com) maintained by her publisher, HarperCollins, includes a wealth of information about Kingsolver, but it also includes a series of "Topics for Discussion," specifically concerning *Poisonwood* (along with her other works). In addition simply typing Kingsolver's name in any browser connects with many useful websites, most of which are directly concerned with *Poisonwood.* Wagner-Martin (2004) includes several Web pages in her biography of Kingsolver (p. 134).

As well as the highly accessible and well-researched biography, Wagner-Martin (2001) offers her *Barbara Kingsolver's The Poisonwood Bible: A Reader's Guide.* This work is primarily designed for assisting students and teachers who wish to read the novel for formal study. Although it is not as detailed as her biography of Kingsolver, Wagner-Martin does include some biographical information before addressing the novel and its critical and popular success, ending with additional suggestions for exploring the novel. This guide might be valuable as part of a classroom set to support students when they study *Poisonwood* as an extracurricular project. As we continue to seek ways to implement the interactive qualities of the Internet, teachers might use Wagner-Martin's *Reader's Guide* as an opportunity to introduce students to the "Customer Reviews" threads that often run beneath book information on amazon.com. The reviews are somewhat informal, but they often include conflicting responses to works and show the reading and responding as a vibrant thing.

Snodgrass (2004) also provides teachers and students with a valuable resource for studying Kingsolver in general and *Poisonwood* specifically, *Barbara Kingsolver: A Literary Companion.* The book is an encyclopedic listing of virtually every topic or detail a reader, student, or teacher might need concerning Kingsolver, and its Appendix A presents a wonderful chronology of *Poisonwood,* support we all need when weaving the narrative of the novel together as we seek coherence as readers. The chronology includes the details of the novel but also inserts historical and biographical details that support framing the novel in the context of history and Kingsolver's life and career. Appendix B is a rich source for teachers as well since here Snodgrass suggests 46 topics for research and writing assignments; this appendix is not exclusively about *Poisonwood,* but it does focus heavily on this novel.

CONNECTION

If students have studied *The Bean Trees* and explored the possible political and historical readings of Kingsolver's work (see Chapter Three), then *Poisonwood* is an ideal opportunity to open that critical lens further: "*The Poisonwood Bible* is her work most obviously indebted to the insights and theories based on the ideas of Karl Marx and his co-writer Friedrich Engels," explains DeMarr (1999) in her "A Marxist Reading of *The Poisonwood Bible*" (pp. 141–144). DeMarr's Marxist lens is a wonderful model for students who are still developing the ability to manage several critical perspectives without allowing their own beliefs to interfere with such analytical dexterity. Most students new to multiple critical perspectives will struggle with terms such as "Marxist," which often has unfortunate connotations for Americans, who associate it with the most negative aspects of modern communist states. DeMarr's Marxist reading of the novel helps show students that a critical lens should be relatively independent of the student's own beliefs. A Marxist reading helps us understand what Kingsolver intends to express *whether we agree with her or not.* The ultimate goal of the literary critic is to unravel what artists are saying before making any pronouncements on those messages. I have watched many AP students destroy the credibility of their literary analysis by expressing their ideas on the topic in a text instead of clarifying what the author has expressed about the topic. Kingsolver clearly expresses a Marxist worldview so students need to be able to analyze that effectively rather than praise or refute those views.

Pulling a popular novel into the classroom can be highly successful because the resources for that novel are readily available. *The Poisonwood Bible* certainly has ample support for teachers and students who wish to move beyond reading the work as a fan to reading the work as a student.

Confronting Africa, Narration, and Biblical Allusion—Multinovel Units

Studying the novel in high school or college English classes is a long-standing tradition. Students expect such class projects, and they probably have a fairly structured expectation of *how* that will occur. As I have mentioned earlier, I believe we have to address the study of novels in our classrooms cautiously with a primary concern for avoiding reducing any novel to a set of details to be memorized by students and authorized by the teacher. In this section, I want to discuss adding multinovel units to the English classroom; this structure moves a great deal of the responsibility for learning to the students and creates a thematic focus for the unit that moves beyond details to concepts raised by the literature.

Wagner-Martin (2004) acknowledges that the success of *Poisonwood* brought numerous comparisons between Kingsolver and a wealth of other highly regarded writers and well-respected novels. Here, I will explore three broad multinovel units that focus on novels of Africa, narrative technique, and biblical/literary allusion. The novels of Africa will include with *Poisonwood* several major works—Chinua Achebe's *Things Fall Apart* (identified in Kingsolver's "Author's Note" to *Poisonwood*), Joseph Conrad's *The Heart of Darkness,* and Alice Walker's *The Color Purple* (although not set in Africa, Paul Theroux's *The Mosquito Coast* is an excellent novel connection dealing with the darkness of the human heart, as well). A second unit pairs *Poisonwood* with William Faulkner's *As I Lay Dying* as a focus on the internal narrative techniques shared by the works (Wagner-Martin, 2004, pp. 48, 107). The third unit will explore the power of biblical and literary allusions as they run through *Poisonwood* and Nathaniel Hawthorne's *The Scarlet Letter.*

Along with being a challenging and rich approach to studying the novel, a multinovel unit can provide teachers with a platform for making the transition from the required, whole-class novel study that tends to be teacher centered to novel studies that are independent projects for students (see the discussion below concerning David Revan's use of *Poisonwood* with his AP class as summer reading). Managing a single whole-class novel assignment is far easier than managing a class of students who are all reading different works. A transitional assignment might include offering a class a set of novels to study that focus on a unifying theme and giving students a chance to choose among those novels. Here, we will look at studying a unit on novels related to Africa, including Kingsolver's *Poisonwood,* Chinua Achebe's *Things Fall Apart,* Joseph Conrad's *The Heart of Darkness,* and Alice Walker's *The Color Purple.* One approach might be to:

- Introduce students to Africa, colonialism, or other related topics in a teacher-directed mini-lesson. This could include "The Vibrations of Djoogbe" (*High Tide in Tucson*)," Web-based activities, or videos on Africa.

ENTRY POINT

The fact-based movie *Endurance* (1999) on 1996 Olympic runner Haile Gebrselassie offers students a moving and vivid entry point into life in Africa. While we want to avoid characterizing an entire continent with a hugely varied array of cultures in any monolithic way, the movie does provide a rich account of Ethiopian life and an opportunity to discuss the complexity of other cultures. It forces the viewer to reconsider assumptions about the people of Ethiopia and Africa. If course time does not allow viewing the entire movie, you might want to select brief scenes to share, notably the early scenes of his life as a boy, when he ran to school and back each day and suffered punishment at both ends for his tardiness and laziness (according to the teacher and his father) although the viewer sees only an amazing child.

- Next, each novel in this unit should be briefly introduced through handouts, multimedia formats such as PowerPoint, or Web-based searches so that students have ample information in order to decide which novel to select for their primary study.
- Divide either a class or several classes into an expert group for each novel; each group will take responsibility for studying one of the novels. Here, you must decide if and how you will ensure that all of the novels are assigned to a group. Students can submit their top two or three choices (students should express the reasons for their choices), and then the teacher can organize the groups according to the size of the class and other factors—Will you have all four novels studied in one class or over several classes that will have a chance to interact with each other?
- Once the introductions have been completed and students assigned to expert groups, you must design a structure for students to study and report on each novel. I have found that students need more support for managing their study than we might suspect (Thomas, 2003). You must establish how long each part of the study will take (reading and research, working as a group to discuss and analyze the novel, and reporting the research and analysis to the rest of the class or other classes), how students will document and report their work within the group and individually, how each group and each student will be assessed, and how (or even whether) students will be held responsible for the four novels they are not required to read and study. There exists a huge range of possibilities in each situation above, but I do believe that these issues must be addressed regardless of how you might choose to handle them.

This multinovel unit on Africa may best be anchored by the group studying Chinua Achebe's *Things Fall Apart;* in fact, the unit might have all students read this novel or *Poisonwood* as an anchor novel with the remaining works divided among the groups. However you structure the unit, students need to be aware of the political and philosophical concerns that Achebe and Kingsolver raise concerning the portrayal of Africa and African culture by those outside the continent. While a primary purpose of this multinovel unit is to shift the analysis and learning responsibility from the teacher to the students, we can enter the unit knowing that several thematic and political issues are common among the works; they include:

- The portrayal of African culture, particularly as it compares and contrasts with American and European culture.
- The role of religion, mythology, and belief in cultures. (Consider revisiting or introducing Joseph Campbell and Bill Moyers' *The Power of Myth,* as noted in Chapter Three, for this topic among the novels.)
- The geography and "place" of Africa.

ENTRY POINT

Discussing Kingsolver's essay, "Paradise Lost" (*High Tide in Tucson*), Wagner-Martin (2004) praises the piece for revealing Kingsolver's own emerging realization about "the power of words—especially the power of metaphor" (pp. 19–20). This essay is an excellent way to show students how Kingsolver attaches meaning to the place of Africa. "It was as deep and edible as Eden," Kingsolver writes, weaving metaphor, biblical allusion, and the significance of place neatly into eight words (p. 114). This power of language blossoms with even greater force in *Poisonwood.*

- The metaphorical and literal value in the journey.
- The contrasts and parallels between Western civilization and tribal life.
- Expectations for males and females in varying cultures.
- Cultural perceptions of good and evil, along with the cultural perceptions about the basic nature of humans.
- The history and impact of colonialism on the oppressors and the oppressed.
- The dynamics of family politics—spouses, siblings, the family unit versus the outside world.
- The value and danger in technology and progress, especially when introduced into "primitive" cultures. (Of course, students should confront the assumptions of "progress" and "primitive" as defined by Western culture.)

These four novels have many additional connections, but my purpose with a unit such as this is to have students tease out those connections and such on their own; the unit is one of discovery. To give the unit cohesion, however, we can take some of the themes above and provide each group with a common set of questions to be answered so that all groups have some commonality in their presentations that can create the larger understandings developed when the groups interact.

CONNECTIONS

For more mature students, the movie, *Apocalypse Now Redux* (1979), would make an excellent connection for a study of the darkness of the human heart. The movie is thematically derived from *The Heart of Darkness* and depends on a journey motif that is parallel to most of the works in this multinovel unit. The movie is quite graphic in language and violence as well as themes, it would have to be targeted to mature students or offered as an extracurricular unit of pursued by student choice and with parental consent at the high school level. The motifs and essential themes of the movie pair well with Conrad's novel, of course, but they also fit with *The Mosquito Coast* and *Poisonwood* in many significant ways. Again, a video allows sharing brief scenes, particularly the river scenes, to make direct connections and dramatic effects relevant to any novel study.

As Wagner-Martin (2004) notes, *Poisonwood* depends on a complex and sophisticated narrative structure that appears to be influenced by that of such books as William Faulkner's *As I Lay Dying* (p. 107). The narration rotates throughout the novel through the four daughters—Rachel, Adah, Leah, and Ruth May—and the mother, Orleanna. The internal monologues of the characters notably omit the voice and thoughts of the father, Rev. Nathan Price, and report from the perspectives of the women on the other men in the story. As a paired-novel unit, *Poisonwood* and *As I Lay Dying* are ideal for the classroom. The unit itself can approach many objectives, including the following:

- The impact of narration on a work of literature.
- Characterization and the portrayal of character through internal monologues and the perceptions of other characters.
- Narrative and novel structure as they contribute to meaning.
- The dynamics and politics of the family unit.
- The use of religious allusions and religious imagery.
- The perspectives of the South, of Americans, and of the world.

A novel unit pairing two novels, as compared with the four-novel unit above, gives the teacher a number of options. These two novels may work well as back-to-back units in which all students read both novels—possibly studying one in class in a fairly traditional way, followed by students reading the second as an independent project. You can use a study of *As I Lay Dying* to lay the groundwork for students exploring *Poisonwood* on their own, particularly since the language of Kingsolver's novel is somewhat more accessible for students than in Faulkner's work (though I wouldn't want to imply that *Poisonwood* is any less sophisticated as a novel).

CONNECTION

An interesting and unusual study of *As I Lay Dying* is a fictional critical exploration of the novel by Wright (1990), *Recalcitrance, Faulkner, and the Professors: A Critical Fiction.* This work allows students to confront Faulkner's novel, but it also pushes the boundaries of critical analysis while utilizing the many critical lenses we hope to foster in our students. This critical work is excellent for college English courses, particularly for students who intend to major in English.

Studying two novels with similar narrative structures and motifs could be managed similarly to the multinovel unit, dividing the class in two and having each half be responsible for only one novel. Again, when students study novels to gain greater sophistication as a reader and a student, the teacher's main goal is to support the study instead of providing what students should gain from the novels. The ways in which students share what they learn (and how they go about exploring the novel) will have a great impact on the effectiveness of the unit. Asking that students determine how they will submit their work adds an additional layer of responsibility to the unit. I suggest requiring students to include these elements in their work:

- Scholarly, properly documented research that includes references from traditional sources (books and journals found in the school or local libraries) and from electronic sources (the Internet, library searches performed electronically with interlibrary loan services). This element requires documentation and provides opportunities for students to evaluate the quality of sources instead of simply gathering a certain number of sources.
- Assignments that reflect both group and individual contributions. The teacher must directly address the fact that group assignments reflect actual collaboration of group members, not simply patching together several individual assignments.
- Assignments that involve composing and performances. In our English courses, students should be involved in reading and writing with virtually all work. We also need to stress that they begin to see multimedia formats as literacy, stressing the need to communicate *more effectively* through that media. If a group prepares a PowerPoint presentation, we must hold it accountable for using that

medium to enhance the presentation in ways that traditional essays would not.

- Thematic analysis with a critical component. Literary analysis should be seen by students as a way of confronting assumptions. Both *Poisonwood* and *As I Lay Dying* offer students many opportunities to question their own and society's expectations and assumptions. Students as literary scholars should be skeptical—instead of striving to comply with a predetermined conclusion about the works.

The third multinovel unit I suggest with *Poisonwood* is pairing the novel with Nathaniel Hawthorne's classic, *The Scarlet Letter.* Both novels are highly dependent on biblical and literary allusion. While teaching *The Scarlet Letter* by itself, I have had the best success with using the biblical allusions running throughout the novel as the primary vehicle for exploring the novel (see Figure 3). The Bible serves as a key source for both novels (as it does in *The Color Purple* and *The Mosquito Coast*), as do the roles of religious leaders in foreign and even hostile lands (the Puritans dealing with the New World and missionaries facing non-Christian traditions in Africa). While the Bible is a highly specific type of allusion, literary allusions also play a large role in *Poisonwood.*

Figure 1 : Questions for Discussions

The Scarlet Letter, Nathaniel Hawthorne

1) In Chapter III, a citizen remarks to Chillingworth, "Of a truth, friend, that matter remaineth a riddle, and the Daniel who shall expound it is yet a-waiting." Explain the significance of this statement in light of Daniel 5. What is the irony here?
2) In Chapter V, Hawthorne uses the expression "brow of Cain" in describing Hester. Read Genesis 4:15 and explain how the biblical passage applies to Hester. What is gained by this comparison?
3) What is the "bar of final judgment" mentioned in Chapter V? What does this contribute to the tone of the novel?
4) In Chapter VI, Hawthorne refers to Puritan childrearing practices and mentions methods used with "Scriptural authority." Discuss some of the Puritan beliefs about raising children. Read Proverbs 13 and cite a passage that may have provided biblical authority for the Puritans' practices. Is the scripture manifested in Hester's raising of Pearl? Explain. What does this biblical reference add to the mood of the novel?
5) Chapter VI also contains a reference to Pearl as "an infant worthy to have been brought forth in Eden." Based on your reading and knowledge of the creation stories in Genesis, explain what you think Hawthorne meant.
6) In Chapter VIII, the governor says, ". . . we might have judged that such a child's mother must needs be a scarlet woman, and a worthy type of

her Babylon." What do you think he means? (See Revelation 17: 1–5 for help.) What is the governor, perhaps ironically, overlooking in his condemnation?

7) Pearl is referred to in Chapter VI as being "of great price." Read Matthew 13: 45–46. How does this allusion suggest both similarity and contrast?
8) John the Baptist is mentioned in Chapter VIII when the author describes Governor Bellingham: "The wide circumference of an elaborate ruff . . . caused his head to look not a little like that of John the Baptist in a charger." Read Mark 6; 1–28 and explain the similarity between the scriptural image of John and the novel's image of Bellingham. Why is the comparison appropriate? What does it add to the tone, if anything?
9) In Chapter IX, Chillingworth says, " . . . it is thus that a young clergyman is apt to speak. Youthful men, not having taken a deep root, give up their hold on life so easily! And saintly men, who walk with God on earth, would fain away, to walk with him on the golden pavements of the New Jerusalem." What is the New Jerusalem of which this person speaks? (See Revelation 21:2.) What is the irony of the remark? What does this tell you about Chillingworth?
10) The story of David and Bathsheba plays an important part in the novel. Refer to Chapter IX and examine the description of the tapestries. What are they like? Read II Samuel 11–12 and explain the similarities between the scriptural account and the novel. Why do you think Hawthorne chose the David-Bathsheba story in connection with the tapestries instead of some other Bible story? What does this contribute to the mood of the novel?
11) In Chapter XI, Hawthorne refers to Enoch by showing how the people of the community feel about their minister. Read Genesis V: 21–24 and explain the significance of the Enoch situation.
12) How is Hester's acknowledgment of her act before the public similar to Psalms 32:5? How is her bearing a child out of wedlock like Psalms 51:5? How is her penance related to II Corinthians 7:10?
13) What similarities do you witness between Dimmesdale's hidden sin and James 4:17? Proverbs 15:13? How is his high community standing (and his inner torment) related to Psalms 62:9 and Ecclesiastes 5:8?
14) What connections can you find between Genesis 4:12, Numbers 32:13, and Roger Chillingworth?

CONNECTIONS

As DeMarr (1999) explains, "Allusions to the poems of Emily Dickinson are particularly prominent" in the narrations of Adah, the literary voice of the novel much as Darl is in *As I Lay Dying* (p. 137). Both "Hope is the thing with feathers" and "Because I could not stop for death" are mentioned by Adah, along with direct references to "Miss Emily Dickinson" in her chapters (pp. 55, 185, 365). As journal prompts, essay topics, or discussion points, students can connect how these allusions support the novel and the characterization of Adah. Also, Adah quotes the entire "The red wheelbarrow" by William Carlos Williams (p. 170). The poem by Williams confronts the clichéd image of the family farm, and it also raises a question about dependency—all relevant to the discussion of *Poisonwood.*

As I will discuss later in more detail, this novel pairing can highlight how both authors confront religious and social assumptions. Additionally, *Poisonwood* can help students see that issues raised in *The Scarlet Letter* continue to hold relevance today as many of the concerns raised by Hawthorne are echoed by Kingsolver; students can begin to establish concerns over religious certainty (such as the arrogance of Rev. Dimmesdale and Rev. Price) and religion's contributions to oppression.

I have suggested three possible novel units that deal with *Poisonwood* as part of multinovel or paired-novel units. The concept of studying pairs of novels or several novels at once can be an effective instructional approach, particularly if your goal is to move the responsibility for learning to the students. The popularity of *Poisonwood* makes it an ideal novel to use when you are expecting students to read and analyze a work with a minimum of teacher input (or coercion).

Confronting the Craft in "Things"

Much of our time in English class is spent studying literature for meaning and purpose; obviously, we study literature as part of the reading curriculum in English from high school into college. A key element of literature study should be studying and practicing the craft of writing. Kingsolver is a supreme craftsperson; her fiction, nonfiction, and poetry stand as superior models of linguistic purpose and control. The meticulous craft in her writing carries the same fluidity and seeming natural ease that we find in William Carlos Williams writing a one-sentence poem about a farm scene; the writing appears at first glance to be something that anyone could have dashed off, but with a closer look, the ideas and expression dazzle.

Emily Dickinson and William Faulkner often dominate the English class, but these writers, as much as I adore their work, often suggest to students that writers strive to be *obscure* instead of clear. My students over the course of twenty years, whether they were ninth graders or adult graduate students (most of whom have been teachers themselves), have confessed that the writers we study in school suggest that good writing is complex—a puzzle to be unraveled by clever readers (usually only something a teacher can decipher). It takes a great deal of sophistication before a reader sees that Dickinson and Faulkner (and Joyce and Eliot) *are* clear, but rarely do high school or college students have that sophistication or patience (and some of the greats *are* purposefully obscure and difficult, we must admit). Kingsolver, however, writes beautifully, with craft and the type of clarity that students can understand—much as they see the craft and clarity in Martin Luther King, Jr., for example. The greatest advantage of Kingsolver as a model for student writers is that she exemplifies both craft and accessibility.

Regardless of how you implement *Poisonwood* in your class, I have had a great deal of success focusing a craft lesson dealing with students as writers around the opening section in "Book One: Genesis" of *Poisonwood*—"The Things We Carried." During the first seventy or so pages of narration in the novel, a carrying motif unifies the four narrations. The Price family members are forced to wear layers of extra clothing and to hide possessions on their persons to avoid weight restrictions on their luggage when they fly from the United States to Africa. The scenes are comic and loaded with implications; in Leah's opening narration, she notes, "My father, of course, was bringing the Word of God—which fortunately weighs nothing at all" (p. 19). Any passage from this opening section can lead to a discussion of using details for purpose in your writing.

CONNECTION

A companion text for this activity might be Tim O'Brien's *The Things They Carried.* The guiding motif of this semiautobiographical novel of Vietnam is reflected in the carrying motif of the title and the opening section of his book. Early in the opening section, the narrator explains, "the things they carried were largely determined by necessity" (p. 2)—paralleling the motivation behind the luggage hidden on the Price family flying to Africa. Students can use passages from O'Brien as a model of a parallel technique although the two works vary in many other ways.

A craft lesson on using details with purpose in student writing can address many other aspects of composition instruction. Some of the objectives and concerns of this lesson include:

- Details, notably objects and brand names, can contribute to associations people already have with those details in a popular sense. "Betty Crocker" is mentioned by Leah on the first page of her first narration (p. 14). While some students may not get the association, we can provide for them the association of Betty Crocker with homemaking, with the traditional housewife. A key concept I share with students is that writers use techniques for one of two reasons—either to reinforce an idea or to contrast with that idea. In other words, writers implement technique in direct and in indirect (or ironic) ways. As the novel develops, Kingsolver clearly confronts the stereotypical and biblical expectations of the wife. Betty Crocker as a mere detail gains significance throughout. Later in the opening section, Leah declares, "Betty Crocker cake mix let us down" (p. 65). Also note the irony of Leah's comment about the "Word of God" being weightless, as well.

- That first point—details often carry meaning that is cultural, temporal (connected with the time in which it is situated), and static (a heart suggests love, for example)—should be contrasted with a second lesson about details. Writers often implement details throughout a work and create meaning for those details, meaning that is unique to that text. In other words, the meaning works from the text out to the reader (whereas the first example suggests that some details have meaning connected to them from the outside in—the meaning lurks within both the detail *and* the readers within their culture). This process might even manipulate details that also carry cultural meaning. In *Poisonwood,* the Bible and snakes are manipulated details as they both gain unique meaning in the story and carry cultural baggage as well. Also in the opening section, the characters learn, along with the reader, that their conceptions of what to carry were flawed; the mother concludes, "We brought all the wrong things" (p. 65). We might ask students how the "Word of God" evolves in meaning for the characters and the reader throughout the novel, for example.
- Because the novel deals with a wide range of time, students can begin to associate the use of details as a device for establishing setting. The product references that run throughout the novel, often in the narrations of Rachel, place the novel in the popular American culture of the mid-1900s. Students who are novice writers tend toward the overt and often struggle with distinguishing the subtle from the arcane. The use of details is one of the many strategies adept writers employ to fulfill the classic quality of excellent writing—showing, instead of telling. In Ruth May's first narration, she says, "Jimmy Crow says that, and he makes the laws" (p. 20); throughout the novel, Kingsolver reveals time, and develops characterization, through the details of the characters' narrations.
- The detail that is often very interesting to students, a detail that fiction writers enjoy manipulating, is the use of names. "If you assign the wrong names to things, you could make a chicken speak like a man. Make a machete rise up and dance," Adah decides, offering an excellent starting point for having students write with the use of names in mind (p. 213). One of the favorite books I keep in my classroom is a baby name book that provides the meanings of names. Students love this book. What do the names of characters

mean? How do the names of characters and historical figures matter in the novel? How are the names of products important?

As mentioned in Chapter Two, reading-like-a-writer activities and craft lessons are powerful tools in developing students both as readers and as writers (Thomas, 2005). The richness and appropriateness of the texts selected as models are key to these approaches. Kingsolver, especially paired with O'Brien, offers accessible and vivid models for students to mine for their own purposes as writers.

Confronting Students as Independent Readers—The Novel outside Class

Simply put, class time is never enough to accomplish all that we wish to pursue as English teachers. A valuable approach to more fully realizing all that we hope to accomplish is the independent novel assignment. While research on learning and literacy points time and again to the importance of choice in literacy learning, we often limit *choice* to what students read. Here, I want to explore assigning all students the same outside reading, *The Poisonwood Bible* but allowing them to choose what they do beyond the actual reading of the novel. I also want to discuss the advantages of the outside assignment. Assigning *The Poisonwood Bible* for outside reading has these elements and advantages:

- Key to this outside novel assignment is taking some in-class time to create interest in the novel and to provide background information. Students are often better and more engaged readers if they read critical discussions of literature first. DeMarr (1999) offers a critical discussion of *The Poisonwood Bible* that is accessible and interesting. Aspects of the novel that will require background information include Belgian involvement in the Congo during the late 1950s and early 1960s, geographical and map sources concerning the Congo during the setting of the novel, information on missionary work and families, and some framework of the unique literary elements of the novel—notably the shifting narrative focus.
- While all students are asked to read the same novel, a primary goal of this type assignment is to ask students to *choose* what they will do with the novel. Outside novel assignments should support students becoming self-directed readers and learners; these assignments should also support the pleasure of reading and the sense of accomplishment that comes from ownership of reading. If we ask students to study a novel outside of class, we should challenge them to reconsider what they believe to be appropriate responses to literature, pushing themselves beyond traditional school-based considerations of literature.

- As I mentioned earlier, an enemy of both students and teachers is time. Outside novel assignments should allow students a longer period of time to complete than the traditional few weeks spent in classroom considerations of novels. Living with a novel allows students to go more deeply into all the contexts of fine literature; as well, extended time provides students with an opportunity to discover what type of readers they are. Weekly book talks or other such structures (Could students form their own extracurricular book clubs, meeting at a local coffee house or bookstore?) can be implemented for five or ten minutes in class to keep the students focused and to encourage sharing.
- As scholars and as lovers of literature, readers often reread novels. If coordinated among an English department, an outside reading and *re*reading of *The Poisonwood Bible* can be used to introduce students to the values of rereading that class time cannot allow.
- *The Poisonwood Bible* serves as an ideal extracurricular novel assignment as well, as Wagner-Martin (2001) has written a guide for readers or companion to the novel. This sort of support may be valuable depending on the experience and sophistication of the students.

STUDENT INSIGHT

Students enrolled in David Revan's Advanced Placement Literature and Composition course read *The Poisonwood Bible* as an outside project for their summer reading prior to their AP course. Once in school, Revan had students write simulated AP exam responses. He then allowed the novel and samples time to sit; later in the semester, the class began to discuss the novel more deeply and fully during class time. As a final activity, Revan created several simulated written response prompts from Kingsolver's novel. The students wrote one-draft responses in a timed setting (30–40 minutes); the following samples reveal the complexity of the novel along with the high level of engagement by the students with the work:

Ruth May, the youngest and seemingly most beloved child of Orleana, is bitten by a Green Mamba snake and dies in the Congo. When Nathan's only response to his own daughter's death was "she wasn't baptized yet," the reader knows Orleana has made her decision silently and perhaps unsurely, but defiantly. She would take her children out of the Congo. The opposing side won over to final victory. Orleana realizes that her priority of fruitlessly trying to keep her broken family together cost her a precious Price.

Lindsey Oliver

I wonder how many other mothers have these two contrasting ambitions today. Orleana's dealing with these two forces also affects the makeup of her family throughout the whole book. The children and Nathan are more content when Orleana feels obligated to them, and not so happy when they have to pick up the slack while she's in bed. . . . All Orleana knows is motherhood yet she still dreams of something more.

Meredith Hutchins

In her monologue, Rachel finds herself conflicted but derisive of her current situation in the Congo. She is torn between the necessities of life in the Congo and the desire to live like she could back in Georgia. . . . Rachel wants the meat the hunt provides, but she does not want to acknowledge the things—like death and blood—that come along with it in her life in the Congo. . . . Rachel is conflicted because she will not let go of the preconceptions and racism of her past to accept the requirements of her current life.

Ben Sloan

The gruesome imagery illustrates Leah embracing African culture and Rachel's disgust toward it. Rachel wants to live in a perfect world, one without famine, death, dirt, world power issues, and disease. She could not stand to be at the hunt so she "went straight back down the burned-up hill and marched all the way home without even telling Mother I was leaving. I am seventeen years old, after all, not a child, and I alone will decide the fate of my life." . . . Rachel only thinks of herself and only cares about herself. She is dying inside just as the animals are.

Jennifer Rook

Adah has always seen the bigger picture and through her realization that virus and man have a partnership in life, she is able to come to terms with her beliefs, and adopts medicine and science as her new faith and devotes time and effort into them and leaves God behind in the dust.

Amy Robertson

Orleana's body is trapped in the Congo while her heart flees to the comfort of Georgia. In her mind, the Congo represents danger, uncertainty, and unhappiness, while Georgia stands for security, safety, and the happiness of herself and her four daughters. This constant mind-battle, however, begins to weigh Orleana down.

Margaret Ann Mabry

Do you ever just want to go home? Do you ever just want to run away? You must. Everyone does. You cannot go home or run away because you are obligated to fulfill your own responsibility. Orleana Price in *The Poisonwood Bible* is torn between two compelling desire: stay in the Congo and protect her family—or—run away from the Congo and protect her family—or—run away from the Congo and flee back to Georgia, her home.

Grier Parrott

Advanced high school or college-level English students can respond with a great deal of sophistication to *Poisonwood;* the novel is complex and engaging, providing an ideal work for students to study on their own as an avenue to greater literary sophistication and personal empowerment.

Confronting the World—Religion, Colonialism, Genocide

"The political themes, concerning genocide and colonialism, are predominant" in *Poisonwood,* explains DeMarr (1999, p. 134). Possibly, we can say that Kingsolver's most popular novel is also her most ambitious, confronting powerful themes such as religion, colonialism, and genocide. Thematically, it certainly is no meek novel.

Our students have one perspective of the United States flexing its military might in Kuwait and, more recently, in Iraq. American patriotism and our pride in spreading freedom throughout the Middle East are central motifs of contemporary life for American teens and young adults. The British and Belgians may have felt the same when they offered civilization to "less" civilized cultures throughout the eighteenth and nineteenth centuries.

ENTRY POINT

Richard Attenborough's *Gandhi* includes several scenes that could introduce students to the British and to the African and Indian perspectives concerning colonialism. One notable scene is an early meeting between Gandhi and British officials in which the British officials reveal their myopic view of the world, their belief that the entire world centers on England. The earlier scenes of Gandhi in Africa are also highly relevant for introducing students to Africa's long history of oppression by more powerful outside forces.

While studying *Poisonwood,* students can gain historical insight as well as begin to confront "questions about truth, justice, colonialism, and genocide" (DeMarr, 1999, p. 133). We should ask students to consider the actual events surrounding the novel, Belgium relinquishing power over the Congo, but we should also allow them to ask questions concerning *any* powerful country imposing its will over a people. "Who should make these decisions for a people?"—our students should ask this question, whether we are discussing the Congo and Belgium or the rise of democracy in a war-torn Iraq.

Possibly the most accessible avenue to such considerations for students are the powerful African characters who begin to populate the narrations of the Price women. Yes, this novel is primarily the vision of the Price daughters and their mother, but their views of the world evolve as they grow more a part of Africa and the people of Africa, notably several male characters who begin to imprint the daughters in ways that Nathan Price has not and cannot. The relationship that develops between Leah and Anatole can serve as a key focus for exploring the growing conflicts in the daughters and in the Price family concerning politics, religion, and an American view of the world. DeMarr states that Leah, "[a] revolutionary and Marxist like her husband, . . . is part of Africa," suggesting that she has rejected the politics and religion bred in her by Nathan Price and America (p. 130).

CONNECTION

Political, economic, and religious systems all share histories of oppression. Students often have difficulty seeing beyond the systems within which they have lived most of their young lives. Provincialism is a quality young people share, and rightfully so. *Poisonwood* confronts a huge number of situations that reveal the oppression of people in a variety of circumstances. Contemporary Americans have seen the horrifying effects of the backlash of people who feel unfairly oppressed (whether their perception is accurate or not, it is how they feel) with the attacks popularly known as 9/11. Anatole, midway through the novel, explains to Leah about the people of the Congo, who have been oppressed by Belgian rule: "'When they are pushed down long enough they will rise up. If they bite you, they are trying to fix things in the only way they know,'" echoing a warning similar to Marx (p. 134). Students should be asked to debate this dilemma, which is also expressed by Langston Hughes's "Harlem" (DeMarr, 1999, p. 134). When people are oppressed, how should they react? Martin Luther King, Jr., and Malcolm X debated this problem according to their conflicting beliefs during the civil rights unrest of mid-twentieth-century America, but this tension knows no time or place—or actually, this dilemma has known all times and places.

Religion, colonialism, and genocide are huge thematic concerns for teachers and students, and we cannot exhaust the possibilities here. That is one of the beauties of *Poisonwood,* its breadth and depth of consideration. But the novel and these themes can offer students a number of opportunities to consider topics such as the following:

- If students have read and discussed Walker's *The Color Purple,* they can once again reconsider the role of missionaries and the politics of religions. These tensions are in Walker's and Kingsolver's work as well as Theroux's *The Mosquito Coast.* For teens and young adults, few opportunities exist to confront the roles of authority figures in their lives and in society, particularly authority figures associated with the central aspects of their lives such as their religion. What happens when belief systems collide? What common ground do belief systems share? How can people of differing beliefs find harmony when power struggles are set aside? What role does judgment play when belief systems interact?
- America has a conflicted history concerning how we view the mixing of politics and religion. When the United States has committed to military action in the MiddleEast—from Kuwait to Afghanistan to Iraq—both the United States and its enemies have invoked their religion during the conflicts. In many situations, the political and military conflicts have been framed as battles between Islam and Christianity. In *Poisonwood,* students can explore how religion, politics, and oppression interact in real and ironic ways.
- Leah and Anatole have rich and dynamic discussions in the middle of the novel that can be used to lead students to consider the complex interactions of the beliefs of any person—about God (or god), about nature, about money, about government, about fairness, and about right and wrong.

I find it difficult to separate the larger themes of the novel because one of Kingsolver's major points is that life is *complex.* For students, the concepts of oppression or colonialism along with terminology such as Marxism or capitalism are brought to life in the characters of *Poisonwood.* If we allow them to pursue these ideas as they are embodied by the characters, then they begin to see how abstractions exist in their own lives—and how their actions impact those ideas.

"The Belgians and American business brought civilization to the Congo! American aid will be the Congo's salvation," Rev. Nathan Price exclaims early in the novel (p. 121). His religious and patriotic arrogance may soon be obvious to our students once they begin to explore the novel closely.

Confronting the Role of Wife and the Role of Women

"'That poor goat of your father's is a very unhappy animal,'" says Anatole to Leah; then she thinks immediately, "*And his wife!*" [italics in original] (p. 284). Although Kingsolver should not be reduced to the stereotypical feminist novelist (Margaret Atwood also sings an unpredictable tune), *Poisonwood* clearly confronts the roles of wife and women, and she leaves very little room for doubt about her views on the oppressive nature of husbands and men. Kingsolver, though, reveals both American and Congolese cultures are oppressive to women through their religion and their cultural expectations.

CONNECTION

Ruth May misnames female circumcision as "Circus mission" (p. 271), revealing a brutal and disturbing custom that at least forces the reader to consider how the Congolese view women (DeMarr, 1999, p. 134). Alice Walker explores the psychological trauma of cultural expectations and female circumcision in *Possessing the Secret of Joy.* Walker's novel is a loose sequel to her popular *The Color Purple,* continuing the character Tashi and her own struggle with the cultural expectations of Africa, expectations that haunt Tashi in disturbing ways.

ENTRY POINTS

Kate Chopin has two stories that are brief and vivid entry points to asking students to reconsider the role of wives and women in society and in marriage, "The Story of an Hour" and "The Storm" (discussed in Chapter Three). In both stories, Chopin asks the reader to confront assumptions about marriage and about wives (and how they view marriage and love and sex). The stories are tightly crafted and engaging for students in high school and college; as well, they are bold arguments that most students will not anticipate. "The Story of an Hour" manipulates irony and how the reader views marriage; "The Storm" offers a shocking twist on infidelity.

Orleanna Price stands as Kingsolver's commentary on the oppression of marriage and Christianity. Early in the novel, Orleanna reminisces:

> Until that moment I'd thought I could have it both ways: to be one of them, and also my husband's wife. What conceit! I was his instrument, his animal. Nothing more. How we wives and mothers do perish at the nads of our own righteousness. I was just one more of those women who clamp

> their mouths shut and wave the flag as their nation rolls off to conquer another in war. (p. 89)

While Kingsolver has clear arguments against traditional expectations for women, wives, and mothers, her use of Orleanna poses an intriguing approach to her argument. Orleanna begins as a devoted woman *of* the religious and cultural mainstream. The reader discovers that World War II changes the Nathan Price she fell in love with, but the novel reveals her eventual disillusionment with the larger issues concerning marriage, womanhood, and religion throughout the novel and through the eyes of Orleanna and her daughters.

The disintegration of the Price family parallels a similar unraveling in Theroux's *The Mosquito Coast;* in both novels, the wives and families begin deeply devoted and even in awe of the father. The fathers of the two novels share only their failures since the father in *Coast* is openly secular, a scientist who taunts the local missionaries in the novel. Rev. Price has no first-person narrative, but he is a formidable presence in all the other narrations because his words drive the lives of all the women of the family.

Kingsolver paints a harsh picture of religion and of husbands and fathers in the novel; students may find this portrayal too harsh to be realistic. What we should ask our students to use the novel as an opportunity to reconsider the politics of marriage and the traditional expectations of wives in modern American society. Have women achieved some level of equality? What roles do marriage rituals play in the status of wives? How do birth control and abortion issues impact the roles of wives and women in general?

While I agree with Kingsolver that the world still tends to oppress women and that organized bodies such as religions continue to subjugate women (with the power of God behind those subjugations), I cannot demand that students reach the same conclusion. The novel may be unfair to Rev. Price and men in general in some ways, but the issues raised must be confronted by students.

More broadly, and portrayed primarily through the daughters, Kingsolver also addresses the roles of women in general. The daughters wrestle with the demons pressed upon them by their father, his religion, and their Southern and American cultures. But the daughters also show a much greater range of problems raised by Kingsolver when compared to the mother, Orleanna. The daughters are bound by their genetics, their family, and their lives as shifted to Africa, but they are also distinct and emerging young women. Each daughter makes decisions about religion, politics, and relationships that are more complicated than Orleanna's single connection with Nathan.

CONNECTION

One of the most intriguing daughters is Rachel, a singularly American young woman smitten by pop culture and her own looks. She may stand as one of Kingsolver's most biting satires of what America does to young women, and the picture is not pretty. A wonderful companion piece to the portrait of the superficial young woman tempted by the dangers of pop culture is Joyce Carol Oates' "Where Are You Going, Where Have You Been¿" Oates' story focuses on Connie, who shares Rachel's egocentrism and lust for pop culture. The short story also wrestles with religious themes. Students often find this story by Oates to be one of their favorites because her style is accessible and engaging, much as Kingsolver's is.

I have touched on many themes and topics as *Poisonwood* is a rich and complex work, but we might be able to say, ultimately, that the novel is supremely a novel about the politics of gender. Kingsolver limits the voices to those of the women to say bluntly that they often are denied a voice—much as Faulkner often gave a voice to the illiterate and the impoverished in his works. Regardless of how much we or our students agree with Kingsolver's feminist stance, the novel forces us to look closely at how men and women have (or do not have) access to power primarily based on the status of their gender.

Poisonwood is clearly the novel now, and possibly forever, that defines Kingsolver the novelist, and it certainly deserves that status. But Kingsolver continues to create wonderful works that are notable in their own right. Let's turn next to *Prodigal Summer,* a novel that takes Kingsolver's reader onto both familiar and unfamiliar ground—with the same magic that makes her work, her work.

ENTRY POINTS AND CONNECTIONS

"The Vibrations of Djoogbe" (*High Tide in Tucson*), Barbara Kingsolver
"Jump-Up Day" (*Homeland and Other Stories*), Barbara Kingsolver
"A Marxist Reading of *The Poisonwood Bible,*" Mary Jean DeMarr (*Barbara Kingsolver: A Critical Companion*)
Endurance (movie), Director Leslie Woodhead
"Paradise Lost" (*High Tide in Tucson*), Barbara Kingsolver
Apocalypse Now Redux (movie), Director Francis Ford Coppola
Recalcitrance, Faulkner, and the Professors: A Critical Fiction, Austin M. Wright
"Hope Is a Thing with Feathers" and "Because I Could Not Stop for Death," Emily Dickinson
"The red wheelbarrow," William Carlos Williams
The Things They Carried, Tim O'Brien

"Harlem," Langston Hughes
Possessing the Secret of Joy, Alice Walker
"The Story of an Hour" and "The Storm," Kate Chopin
"Where Are You Going, Where Have You Been?," Joyce Carol Oates

Chapter Five

Confronting *Prodigal Summer*

Kingsolver begins the "Acknowledgments" that open her novel published in 2000 with, "This novel grew from soil richly blessed by my Virginia friends and neighbors," signaling her continuing artistic concern for place along with a homecoming of sorts (p. ix). Not only does Kingsolver move her fictional world back to U.S. soil from Africa, but she returns to the Appalachian mountains of her birthplace.

Prodigal Summer is a novel as rich in language and characterization as it is by the implications of its title. It also travels into areas of sexuality that her works had previously skirted. While this novel may be best for adult readers, it certainly is a wonderful novel for teachers to embrace, both for themselves as readers and humans and for their classrooms where appropriate. This chapter will spend a bit more time unfolding this novel since teachers will find less material available on *Prodigal Summer* than on *The Poisonwood Bible* or *The Bean Trees.* This chapter will explore as well teachers teaching the novel for its three intertwining stories, using the novel for self-renewal, and unfolding the novel's many rich and varied themes and motifs—farm life, the food chain, sexuality, and the losses of life.

ENTRY POINT

Kingsolver offers us the ideal entry point to her novel with the poem "Prothalamium" by Aaron Kramer. Kramer is described on the Web (www.aaronkramer.com) as a social critic and a poet, suggesting how apt his politics and his verse are for the opening of Kingsolver's novel.

Students can begin with this poem, discussing its unusual title ("prothalamium" means a song honoring marriage) and its natural and seasonal references. This opening activity can help students establish some possible motifs that connect the poem and the novel. As students read and after they complete the novel, they can return to Kramer's poem to confirm or expand their initial analysis of the poem. As the students move into a direct study of the novel, they can also begin to consider the novel's title, *Prodigal Summer,* and its implications and the word "prodigal" and how it impacts the novel.

"Not all political concerns have to be with nations, wars, and ownership," opens Wagner-Martin's (2004) brief analysis of *Prodigal Summer* (p. 115). Her analysis and most of the reviews of this novel gravitate toward the environmentalism that anchors both the questions Kingsolver considers and the politics of her story. Kingsolver has never hidden her scientific concerns that lean toward the biology of existence or her strong social consciousness that includes humans and all creatures populating our planet. With this novel, again, Kingsolver's beliefs are personified and ideas turn into action. We might can imagine that some of the ecological spirit that spoke loudly in the works of Emerson and Thoreau in nineteenth-century America regains its voice with Kingsolver's fiction.

CONNECTIONS

Students will find kindred spirits to *Prodigal Summer* in one of Kingsolver's earlier novels, *Animal Dreams,* and in a classic work of American literature and American thought, *Walden,* by Henry David Thoreau. The ecological and environmental elements of her earlier novel and of Thoreau's classic work are well suited for study as parallel assignments or as follow-up readings after *Prodigal.* Students find it difficult sometimes to equate Thoreau's nineteenth-century concerns with their contemporary worlds. His intense attachment to nature is illuminated by Deanna's affection for the wild in the novel. Regardless of how these works are connected in the classroom, all three provide students with questions about how humans interact with nature and how nature works as a system.

ENTRY POINTS

When we approach *Prodigal Summer* or Thoreau and Emerson for themes concerning the environment or ecology, students in high school and college are often slow to be engaged. Even in rural America, modern life is often greatly disconnected from nature, partly because we are more and more a consumer society and less and less a people who conserve. REM, whose music has been mentioned before, have spoken from a platform similar to Kingsolver's over their career. Two of their songs are ideal entry points to discussions of nature and the environment, "Cuyahoga" and "Fall on Me." "Cuyahoga," suggested in Chapter Three, raises issues of industrial waste and employs a Native American motif; "Fall on Me" has a subtext of acid rain although the song has additional layers not related to environmentalism. Both songs are excellent openings to asking students how they feel about nature and how they feel connected (or disconnected) from nature—and why. Differing student attitudes toward nature might serve classroom discussions well as students begin to explore the conflicting attitudes of characters in *Prodigal* concerning nature, such as between Deanna and Eddie or Garnett and Nannie.

Set in the Zebulon National Forest over three months of summer, this novel offers a hypnotic weaving of three storylines that "though geographically tangential, seem unconnected" (Wagner-Martin, 2004, p. 117). The reader may be mesmerized or disoriented by the opening line concerning the character Deanna Wolfe (who seems to be the main character although the novel refutes the traditional use of a main character in this work, as does Kingsolver herself): "Her body moved with the frankness that comes from solitary habits," the novel begins, seductive and incomplete (p. 1). Soon we come to know the ironically sensual and solitary life of Deanna, whose solitude is disrupted by the oddly named Eddie Bondo. This opening story is driven by the motif "Predators." The second storyline is titled "Moth Love," and it reveals the tragic life of Lusa Maluf Landowski. Deanna works as a ranger in the forest overlooking the farmland where Lusa comes to marry Cole Widener. Lusa trades her university life as an academic doctor conducting research on moths and butterflies for the life of a farmer's wife. "Old Chestnuts" serves as the third narrative lens, detailing the tensions between Garnett Walker and Nannie Rawley.

Kingsolver offers readers, students, and teachers a novel that is rich in plot, characterization, and theme. However, this work is read much less often in classes than are *The Bean Trees* (which has fewer adult issues and less language that might be a problem in high school classrooms) and *The Poisonwood Bible* (which moved into classrooms from the momentum of its enormous and deserved popularity). Let's look now more closely at the three plot lines that interweave throughout the novel, held together by the setting of the work and "the elusive totem of the novel . . . [,] the coyote" (Wagner-Martin, 2004, p. 119).

Confronting Three Stories as One

The narrative structure of this novel allows us to bring *Prodigal* to the classroom and to shift the analysis of the novel into the hands of our students. As the novel has less support material than some of her other works, students are less likely to simply cull their analysis from critical works and summaries provided commercially. Classes can be divided into three study groups, with each group responsible for one of the plot lines. After each group prepares a thorough analysis and understanding of one story, the entire class can share and draw larger connections for the book as a whole. This activity can have the following guiding elements:

- Each group will prepare an explanation for the guiding motif of their section—"Predators," "Moth Love," and "Old Chestnuts." They should look at both what these terms carry in meaning unrelated to the novel and what they come to mean within each storyline.
- Each group will analyze the character pair that stands at the center of each story—Deanna and Eddie in "Predators," Lusa and Cole in "Moth Love," and Garnett and Nannie in "Old Chestnuts." Students should begin to see how Kingsolver creates characters that are fully developed and complex while also being personifications of essential ideas and beliefs (without being mere stereotypes of those ideas or beliefs). Each pairing of characters struggles with basic tensions that define the individuals and their relationships.
- Each group will detail how the coyote matters in each storyline. Students will find the coyote as a dominant element of "Predators" and "Moth Love" but may have a harder time with its significance in "Old Chestnuts." Students might do some additional research on the coyote: Why does Kingsolver include it specifically?
- Each group will outline each separate storyline to help maintain the coherence of each story within the larger novel. I have noticed that some students have difficulty staying engaged with novels that use interweaving techniques. Amy Tan's *The Joy Luck Club* caused this problem for my students. When students have trouble with the narrative weaving, I often offer them the opportunity to read the "Predators" sections together, for example, before coming back to read "Moth Love" and "Old Chestnuts" in the same way. If *Prodigal Summer* is to be studied with a group focusing on each storyline, you might allow students to read the one subplot assigned to them straight through for their group work before reading the whole novel.

Like *Poisonwood,* Kingsolver's narrative technique in *Prodigal Summer* can be challenging to students, but the interweaving stories are almost made more dynamic by the technique. Tan's novel and many works by Faulkner force the reader to hold onto motifs and tone and setting while the linear nature of plot settles into the background. For students, shifting their focus away from primarily being concerned with "what happens" may be a beneficial thing. Before looking more closely at the many dynamic elements of this novel for the classroom, let's consider how *Prodigal Summer* can challenge and renew us as teachers, as readers, and as humans.

Confronting Ourselves as Readers and Teachers

A regrettable fact of being an English teacher is that our work often pushes us further and further away from the reading and writing that probably pulled us into the field. If we teach American literature, we have a cycle to our lives that includes well-loved works by Thoreau, for instance, but we may find ourselves saying "Who¿" when a student mentions a writer born within our lifetime. A recurring plea I have been making throughout the past twenty years is that we must practice our field to be the best teachers we can be. That professional call is joined here by my belief that we must renew ourselves *personally* as well. I recommend that all of you who have not read Kingsolver or have only limited acquaintance with her work, pick up *Prodigal Summer* and have a reading experience—as teacher, as a lover of literature.

Prodigal Summer is the most fully mature work by Kingsolver in terms of content and themes. It challenged me and moved me as few works have. Although we, as teachers, certainly are mature and sophisticated readers, let me offer some suggestions here just to rattle the cage a bit, especially if you are facing the inevitable burnout that plagues our profession:

- Put down your pen or highlighter! My daughter chastises me because I rarely read without annotating—underlining, jotting comments, and highlighting to the point of absurdity. A gift I occasionally give myself is the reading of a book with no writing utensil in reach or sight. The pages of my copy of *Prodigal Summer* were once unmarked. Because I am now writing *about* the book, the pages are more worn, and a few ink stains and vibrant streaks of highlighter have soiled the pages. But it is nothing like my copy of *The Great Gatsby*—thankfully.
- Personal and professional renewal may be a solitary thing, but we often suffer isolation as teachers, which leads to burnout and frustration. Use the reading of *Prodigal Summer* as an opportunity to form a reading club in your department, throughout the faculty, or in conjunction with faculty at other schools. Reading engaging literature

is a wonderful experience; sharing it with others is even more enriching. Kingsolver's own website and several other websites offer discussion questions to focus such a reading group. Although I believe we should sit with our friends to discuss the pleasure of reading, we might form some electronic reading clubs as well around *Prodigal,* although I suggest you find some time to meet face to face when possible.

- Use the reading of this novel to begin or rekindle the writer inside you. Keeping a journal (go buy one at a local book store; you deserve it!) or beginning to submit writing for publication can be spurred by reading rich and beautiful writing. Writing is an act of discovery—much like reading. The reading of *Prodigal Summer* and exploring yourself as a writer can be enriching activities that will benefit you as a person, and they will certainly spill over into your role as English teacher.
- Share the pleasure and excitement you feel while reading the novel with your students. Whether you drop a spontaneous comment about *Prodigal Summer* during class or set aside a few minutes once a week to share yourself *as a reader,* students feed off their teachers' passions. This novel is a novel of passion, and it inspires passion in the reader. Let students see that love and passion as you read for pleasure. A brief reading aloud of a passage that touches you to your classes will serve many goals we seek as English teachers—the type of goals that may be overlooked as we are planning with an eye on standards or high-stakes tests.

I'll leave this discussion with a confession—I love Deanna in *Prodigal Summer,* and I began missing her the moment I completed the novel *for the first time.* Reading a beautiful novel is a present we can give ourselves. But it is also a present we should give our students.

Confronting Sexuality in Literature

As I have noted earlier, I am very much a proselytizer of Kingsolver's works. During summer graduate courses, I began to mention *Prodigal Summer* more and more, often noting the delicate and vivid sexuality of the novel. The class was made up of middle school English teachers who quickly began carrying copies of the novel with them to class each day. I have used the same strategy with high school students and undergraduates; sexually charged literature draws an audience.

I believe my strategy for pulling students to wonderful writers began when my own high school English teacher introduced me to D. H. Lawrence—a bold move that has led me to a life of literature for which I could never thank him enough. This leads to one of the most controversial but valuable elements of *Prodigal Summer*—a frank discussion of the role of sexuality in literature. Just as Kingsolver uses questions to focus her fiction, I often focus my teaching on big questions—What makes poetry, poetry¿, for example.

I have found that one important topic we rarely broach with students is when does explicit sexuality stand as "literature" and when does it become "pornography." This is a key concern for helping students grow as readers, students, and people. Even in our classrooms, we fall victims to making topics taboo, thus something young people laugh about. To avoid this giggle factor, we should address sexuality in literature directly, particularly through rich and vibrant works such as *Prodigal Summer.*

ENTRY POINT

Particularly in high school English classes, addressing controversial subjects may be easier if the writer and the text are established parts of the traditional canon. One work that succeeded for me when I wanted students to consider sexually imagery (as a contrast to graphic sex in lesser literature) was Samuel Taylor Coleridge's "Kubla Khan." As an introduction to sexual imagery, this poem works well with younger students; as a complex poem to challenge more advanced English students, the poem works for them also. The poem allows students to place sexual imagery and language in the context of thematic concerns; in the poem, Coleridge is dealing with nature, inspiration, and creativity, all of which are reinforced by the sexual language and imagery of the incomplete poem. Kingsolver deals with many of the same motifs and themes in her novel, where we can ask students to look at the *intent* of the sexual language and the sexual acts within the larger purposes of a piece of literature.

CONNECTION

"Reader, hear my confession: I have written an unchaste novel"—so begins Kingsolver's "Taming the Beast with Two Backs," which addresses her own struggling with sexuality in literature (p. 222). The allusion of her title suggests that sex is a part of the language and action of *all* literature, including the sacred works of Shakespeare or, even more distant, the bawdy works of Chaucer—both of whom stand as solid parts of the traditional canon. This essay opens the door for students to consider the role of sexual language and references in literature as well as how those concerns weigh on serious writers. Kingsolver confesses her own psychological censor, her mother. But beyond this tension in her as a writer (similar to Hemingway writing letters expressing his fear of including the word "balls" in *The Sun Also Rises*), she also raises a wonderful concern about language in general—that "[t]he language of coition has been stolen—or really, I think, it's been divvied up like chips in a poker game among the sides of pornography, consumerism, and the medical profession" (p. 225). The essay is a wonderful discussion, filled with hesitancies and humor, of sex in literature, but it also confronts the nature of language as it is impacted by culture, economics, politics, and religion. Whether students connect her essay with the novel or simply use it as a way to begin to consider these important issues seems irrelevant in the long run.

Why is sex in Kingsolver "literature," but "pornography" somewhere else?—students surely wonder, if they don't ask directly. This question is part of a bigger issue about language and literature that seems never to be settled completely in our society, a free America with many linguistic taboos. Why is a racial slur okay in Twain or Flannery O'Connor but despised in rap lyrics? How did coarse sexual language in D. H. Lawrence or James Joyce move from pornography to high literature?

English courses are certainly the appropriate places for these considerations despite the controversy inherent in asking the questions. Students will benefit from discussing the *intent* of literature. Why does Kingsolver (or Shakespeare or Joyce) pull the reader into Deanna and Eddie's actual love making? The intent of sexual descriptions or sexual imagery (which is pervasive in literature) is a key element in why we praise some writing and condemn others.

Some activities with *Prodigal Summer* that can lead students to explore sexuality in the novel include:

- Ask students to classify the sexual references throughout the novel—references referring to actual sex acts contrasted with sexual imagery. This helps students begin to distinguish intent, and it provides a valuable experience with literal and figurative language, one of the most important lessons for evolving readers and students.
- While studying the novel, ask students to maintain a log of sexual language in their daily lives—spoken among their peers, in TV shows or commercials, in the text of magazines, in the music they hear. They should be encouraged to consider intent with these examples also, particularly as they begin to see the nature of sexual innuendo in advertising or in casual conversation.
- Have students expand their critical eye and ear to identifying the taboo language of their daily lives. What can they say in one venue but not another, comparing home and school and peer groups. Why are some

words taboo? What power does that give those words?

- Ask students to focus on the character of Deanna. Her sexuality is woven into the nature motifs of the "Predators" narrative, culminating in her own fertility theme.
- Ask students to compose an original work integrating sexual imagery to reinforce a theme or motif of their writing. A passage from the novel can serve as a model for this activity.

Thinking about moths, Lusa believes "[t]hey tell their love across the fields by scent . . . [;] she considered a language that could carry nothing but love and simple truth" (p. 47). For Kingsolver and her characters, much of *Prodigal Summer* is about the larger sexual politics of nature and of words. The novel ends with the power of sexual attraction: "a tug of impalpable thread on the web pulling mate to mate and predator to prey, a beginning or an end," suggesting the essential nature of sexual language within the greater idea of the novel (p. 444).

Confronting Motifs and Themes—Farm Life, the Systems of Nature, and Life's Losses

Wagner-Martin (2004) identifies *Prodigal Summer* as once again a political work, but she calls it "her farmland novel" (p. 120). Here she offers the reader a work as detailed and complex in many ways as *Poisonwood,* although many fail to see it as such. For the classroom, we will look at how *Prodigal Summer* addresses farm life, the systems and patterns of nature, and the inevitable losses of life. If students can read this novel after several of her other novels and many of her essays, they will see how it fits as a culmination of how she has lived and continues to live as a part of her beliefs. If this novel is the student's starting point for the works of Kingsolver, it clearly shows what she wants her reader to question and to do.

Exploring the interaction between humans and nature—and more specifically, the farming life—may seem, ironically, as less than fertile ground for an engaging work of fiction. But Kingsolver breaths life into characters, places them in a natural setting, and watches as tensions and conflicts breed a story, or more accurately, three stories. A farming theme or motif actually carries all three stories, though in differing ways. Deanna, as a ranger, metaphorically farms, or possibly we should say shepherds, the mountainside that overlooks the more literal farmland where Lusa finds herself the widowed owner of a failing farm. Both Garnett and Nannie are farmers, concerned with trees and personal gardens that force them to fight over their natural treasures and that raise for the readers issues of ownership and pesticides.

ENTRY POINT

Adah quotes William Carlos Williams' "The red wheelbarrow" in *Poisonwood,* which deals with the cultural contrasts inherent in the assumptions about farming held by the Price family that fail when Rev. Price ignores farming practices unique to Africa. "The red wheelbarrow" can serve as an entry point for discussing farming in *Prodigal Summer.* The poem and the novel explore how humans "depend" on the land for our essential survival. Since the poem manipulates a few details we associate with the stereotypical farm—chickens, a wheelbarrow, red, white, and rain water—students can use the poem to explore their own knowledge of and ignorance about farms. The poem offers a fairly stark statement that humans do depend "so much" on the farm, but the novel challenges the reader to move beyond that fact to asking what should we do to protect that upon which we depend so much.

The farming motif overlaps with other major themes, as I will discuss later, but it confronts students in a number of engaging ways.

- The "Moth Love" narrative, for example, deals most directly with farming. This aspect of the novel can lead to students researching the current state of family farming as it faces the rising power of corporate farms. Students can research what distinguishes these two types of farming; then they can begin to debate if and why we as a country should protect or preserve the family farm.

CONNECTION

John Gardner's "Redemption" is a short story set on a family farm where a tragic tractor accident leaves one child dead and an entire family shaken to their bones. This story is a wonderful companion to Kingsolver's novel because it is set on a family farm, a parallel to Lusa's story, and it raises essential questions of life, of loss, and of humanity. Gardner's writing is highly moral, much as Kingsolver's works are. As a craftsperson, Gardner has few peers. The complexity of the language and the starkness of the details and tragedy often deeply impact students. The story has a puzzling turn just past the middle that forces the reader to read carefully in order to understand how the story does fulfill the questions it raises in the very first horrifying sentence. As in Kingsolver, Gardner's characters are vivid and engaging, and the reader is filled with questions from the beginning.

- Within the "Old Chestnuts" narrative, Kingsolver interjects a battle over pesticides. Garnett Walker clings to the survival of chestnut trees, possibly representing his clinging to tradition and his own fading past, but he fights with his neighbor, Nannie Rawley, who rebukes chemical pesticides. This conflict can lead to discussions about pesticide use and our stewardship of timberland. The deft characterization of Garnett and Nannie make these arguments and tensions more intriguing since Kingsolver avoids demonizing any of the characters even when we suspect that a character holds views counter to her own. In the novel, as is true in life, the questions and solutions are not so simple.

- Deanna's story, "Predators," is the most metaphorical exploration of "farming," since she serves as a ranger, one who watches over the land and simultaneously lives off the land but doesn't actually farm the land as in the Lusa narrative or even as in Nannie's story. Deanna's story does, however, force the reader to question how humans respond to animals when those animals threaten our own organized attempts at farming the land and tending to livestock. Eddie Bondo wanders into Deanna's space, not unlike the coyote that threatens the livelihood of farmers. The narrative that runs throughout "Predators" begins to ask the reader about our responsibilities for both the domesticated and the wild, whether it be animals or land.

While it is somewhat artificial to separate Kingsolver's themes, I believe students can see that she pushes the novel beyond our human connections with the forests and our farmland and toward the larger systems of nature, of which humans are a part. The predator/prey motif, the food chain motif, is both a motif within the farming theme and one that encompasses the whole of the book. Deanna's ambivalence about nature and the cruelty of nature (if it *is* cruelty) helps create a truly honest exploration of nature that shows how humans are at the mercy of nature while also holding the power to destroy the very nature that keeps humans alive.

The predator/prey motif is developed in various ways throughout the novel. The coyote serves as a central embodiment of Deanna's conflicting feelings about nature, but Eddie Bondo enters her world and sets up a human predator/prey motif that is paralleled in the family politics that surfaces after Cole's death, leaving Lusa as a vulnerable and often naïve target of those who want the farm to remain with the blood kin. This motif as a part of Kingsolver's exploration of the systems of nature also raises one of her favorite topics—ownership. Who owns the forest Deanna patrols? How is the forest different from, or the same as, Lusa's farmland? Is Deanna's commitment to be a steward of the forest different than Lusa's ownership of the farm or Garnett's, of his land, or Nannie's, of her garden and the whole of nature?

Kingsolver's focus on the systems of nature pulls the reader to the widest possible considerations; then she turns to one of the narrowest—humans' connections with humans. Consider these passages from the novel:

> If the thought caused him sadness—that he would never again know the comfort of human touch—he sensed it was merely a tributary to the lake of grief through which an old man must swim at the ends of his days. (p. 135)
>
> Her body ached with the burden of her aloneness. (p. 153)
>
> I wish I could have back every minute we wasted being mad at each other. I wish we'd had time to make a baby together. I wish. [italics in original] (p. 235)
>
> "I think it'd be worse losing the person you love than dying yourself." (p. 241)

A motif of loss runs throughout this novel, ironic against the seemingly optimistic nature of the story. The motif of loss is an undercurrent of many characters' lives, but it is a dominant factor in the life of Lusa, whose husband Cole dies young and tragically. What is Kingsolver searching for with this motif?

The topic of loss can be approached through Gardner's "Redemption," mentioned above, as that story, like Kingsolver's novel, pushes the reader to reconsider and possibly value our human connections even more. The relationships of the novel are often clumsy and even troubling, from the awkwardness of Deanna craving a younger man to Lusa struggling with her sexuality and her desires after the loss of her husband. The many losses that characters feel and experience often stand in contrast to the sexual language and fertility that run throughout all the narratives. The tensions between that fertility and the sadness in the characters over their feelings of solitude are possibly what draw us most deeply to those characters and to their stories.

If our students look closely at these three motifs—farming, the systems of nature, and the losses of life—they can begin to make the larger connection Kingsolver seems to suggest; there is a unity of all things that should be valued by the human race. Through her fiction, Kingsolver brings to life the central concepts of American Transcendentalism espoused in the works of Emerson and Thoreau. Deanna feels her body and heart drawn toward Bondo, who gives her life metaphorically and literally, even as they argue over the sanctity of the coyote, which they view as differently as possible. Lusa, in turn, is given a new life with the loss of her husband's life, a loss that leaves her aching in ways she might not have expected.

"Two years alone had given her a blind person's indifference to the look on her own face," the reader learns early in the novel about Deanna (p. 2). Yet this same woman is deeply connected to every living and nonliving thing on the side of Zebulon Mountain under her watch. How did this disassociation with herself happen? Kingsolver sets out in the novel to show us the value in treasuring both the nature that surrounds us and the people who populate our lives.

For Further Consideration

Prodigal Summer, like all of Kingsolver's works, offers our students and our classrooms a wealth of opportunities for students as readers and as writers. Although this novel has not been included in English classes as often as *The Bean Trees* and *The Poisonwood Bible,* it can lead to many assignments that would benefit our students greatly. Here are a few ideas for further assignments:

- Chapter 22, a "Predators" chapter, introduces the reader to a favorite concern of Kingsolver—words. "Her dad didn't know the word *fledge,* but he knew what it meant," we read about Deanna's father (p. 361). This passage in the first paragraph of the chapter can be the basis for students to consider words, or as we often call this sort of study in school, vocabulary. Students can discuss in groups or through writing in journals or essays the nature of the meaning of words. This discussion can be connected with the discussion of the sexual language I have covered above. What is the importance of precise words? What are the nuances of words, what connotations do words carry? These broad considerations of words are far more important than memorizing a list of words for a multiple-choice or matching test.
- Students in high school and college are keenly interested in relationships. *Prodigal Summer* uncovers a wide range of relationships. Deanna struggles with her attraction to a younger man; Lusa suffers the guilt she feels after being unhappy in her marriage, then losing her husband to a tragic death; and Garnett and Nannie flirt with a relationship late in their lives. Students are eager to write about if and when these characters should pursue their relationships as well as discussing their own ideas about love, sex, and marriage.
- If students have read and discussed Kingsolver's other works, they may be interested in how she views gender roles in *Prodigal Summer.* Students could discuss or write about how this novel continues Kingsolver's commentary on gender roles and how this novel is also unlike her other works.
- *Prodigal Summer* is clearly a work about nature. From coyotes to moths to chestnut trees and the dangers of chemical pesticides, the work brings the reader close to the details of nature. Students could explore how humans care for and mistreat the world around them. What is the current status of coyotes in our country? What

is the role of moths in the ecosystem? How do farmers deal with the threat of pesticides? What alternative farming methods exist and to what degree are those alternatives used by American farmers? Why do organic foods cost more in the grocery stores?

Early in the novel, the narrator states, "She was well accustomed to watching Yankee brains grind their gears, attempting to reconcile a hillbilly accent with signs of a serious education" (p. 11). Just as Deanna seems to disorient those who meet her, Kingsolver's writing rattles her readers' cages. Whether it is the sexual innuendo of Deanna's and Bondo's relationship ("This one had stolen her advantage—he'd seen inside her") or the literal sex inherent in nature ("to live for a day on sunlight and coitus") or the assumptions about ownership that drive Garnett ("a hundred years ago, when his grandfather owned the whole southern slope of Zebulon Mountain"), Kingsolver offers our students a wide range of questions and expects a great deal in return (pp. 3, 16, 82). This is a novel that belongs on our shelves as readers and in our classrooms as teachers.

ENTRY POINTS AND CONNECTIONS

"Prothalamium," Aaron Kramer
Animal Dreams, Barbara Kingsolver
Walden, Henry David Thoreau
"Cuyahoga" and "Fall on Me," REM
"Kubla Khan," Samuel Taylor Coleridge
"The red wheelbarrow," William Carlos Williams
"Redemption," John Gardner

Chapter Six

Confronting Language, Confronting Culture

"Poetry is a different beast," Kingsolver (1998) declares in the introduction to her collection of poetry, *Another America/Otra America* (the introduction that was later reprinted in *Small Wonder* as "Stealing Apples"); "I rarely think of poetry as something I make happen—it is more accurate to say that it happens to me" (p. xv). Although by her own admission, Kingsolver is primarily a novelist, her poetry offers many opportunities in our English classrooms as new sources for discussing poetry and as new ways to explore poetry and becoming a poet.

You can simply add a work or two of Kingsolver's poetry into your classroom because she stands as a vibrant and talented poet who is worthy of inclusion in the canon. In the opening poem of her collection, "Beating Time," Kingsolver laments an actual mandate by the governor of Arizona that eliminated poetry as a requirement in the state's schools. This collection confronts the reader through poetry much as her nonfiction does; it is a decidedly political collection, divided into five sections—"The House Divided," "The Visitors," "The Lost," "The Believers," and "The Patriots"—with all of the poems both in Kingsolver's original English and translated into Spanish by Rebecca Cartes.

"Beating Time," the opening poem, contains vivid language and metaphorical language, and it also raises an interesting debate about what matters in schools—particularly, the place of art in the curriculum. Opening with a direct and literal statement of an act by the governor, Kingsolver sets the political nature and aggressive tone of her poems to follow. This poem, and her entire collection, is suitable for both anaan analytical essay that discusses the poems as a *collection*—determining how the poems work in a unified way to create motifs and themes more broadly.

- A more time-focused full-class activity with Kingsolver's collection is to break the class into five groups, assigning each group one of the sections of the collection. This works well when students come together as a whole to discuss and share what each section creates as a section, followed by the whole class sewing together what each group presents for a larger understanding of the collection. This sort of activity allows you to focus on scholarly group work that requires careful work by the groups and structured sharing of information among groups. That each group is responsible for the other four groups' presentations is a key element to this activity.
- I will discuss the writing of poetry by students later in this chapter, but I want to note here that Kingsolver's collection can help show budding writers that the writing of poetry is not a string of isolated snapshots. Poetic expression often is on a larger scale than school suggests. If the study of a collection of poetry can inspire a student to begin to form a collection over an entire year or over several years, we will have served that student well.
- Because much of critical literary analysis involves determining purpose and associating parts with wholes, we can use a collection of poetry to reinforce those processes. If having students read the entire collection or even having groups deal with separate sections of the collection is too time consuming, we can share the broad motifs of the collection—such as language, politics, alienation, immigration, and activism—with our students through direct instruction, and then we can assign or ask students to choose individual poems from the collection to explore how that single poem contributes to the broader ideas of the book.

CONNECTIONS

Kingsolver herself provides us with a number of opportunities to connect Kingsolver's poems and her collection with several poets. In her "Introduction" and in the opening of each section of the collection, Kingsolver quotes and mentions a number of poets whose poems can be associated with her themes and style. The poems directly quoted include Carolyn Forché's "Ourselves or Nothing," Sharon Olds' "The Eye," and Adrienne Rich's "Storm Warning." She also quotes Walt Whitman and mentions the influence of Lucille Clifton on her perceptions of poetry.

Exploring an entire collection allows students to dig deeply into the richness of poetry, a key element in their evolving understanding of how poetry is distinct from prose. Kingsolver's collection forces them to address whether her argument about two Americas is valid, and it may serve as an introduction to the concept of poetry as a political act. Much of what students believe about all types of literature is grounded in how that literature is presented to them (fragmented in anthologies, selected *for* them) and what we ask them to do with that literature (primarily, traditional critical analysis driven by the teacher's analysis that is then shared with students). Further, students are greatly impacted by our writing assignments. The study of poetry has been profoundly affected by all of these elements. When we bring a new poet or a new approach to poetry into our classrooms, we have an opportunity to empower our students and ourselves in new and dramatic ways. Bringing Kingsolver's collection into our classroom, then, becomes a political act.

Confronting Feminist Poetry

"I am the woman whose flesh/ does not move when she walks," begins Kingsolver's poem "Reveille" (11. 1–2), which explores a topic that has even become a focus of TV series and reality programming, cosmetic surgery. On its own, this poem offers students a chance to explore the poetic nature of free verse in modern poetry and to consider Kingsolver's challenging of modern women's quest to be "painted in the colors of no flower/ that ever really bloomed" (11. 7–8). The poem raises language and cultural argument to the level of poetry through techniques less obvious than simile or meter—loaded and manipulated diction, ethnic and gender references, negating words and word forms ("-less," "no," "not").

CONNECTIONS

A multigenre and multimedia assignment that students enjoy can spring from the poetry of feminism; this unit helps balance the often male-dominated voice of the literature we study and helps broaden our consideration of many texts, including *reading* movies. Kingsolver's "Reveille" along with Marge Piercy's "Barbie doll" and "A Work of Artifice" can introduce a larger unit that deals with how woman are portrayed and viewed in American society. I have often combined a study of Adrienne Rich, Anne Sexton, and Sylvia Plath with the viewing of the movie *Pleasantville* (1999), which includes many of the motifs of feminist poetry through the June Cleaver-type mother in the sitcom town of Pleasantville—how beauty is portrayed and perceived, how makeup and fashion impact women's lives, how cultural expectations impact women's decisions. This unit has proven to be rich and engaging with students, who often have difficulty seeing past the norms of their daily lives. Female students are often quick to defend their use of make-up, for example, arguing that they wear it *by choice* and denying that they could in any way be coerced into wearing it. Particularly through the poems and a wonderful scene in *Pleasantville* (the mother has begun to display color in this black-and-white sitcom; to hide the color, her son helps her apply black-and-white makeup in order to conform), students are more apt to reconsider how social pressures shape the ways that women are viewed and view themselves.

It is difficult to separate Kingsolver the feminist from Kingsolver the political writer; "Reveille" clearly fits within both interests. A natural connection to Kingsolver's poem is the work of Marge Piercy—notably "A Work of Artifice" and "Barbie doll." Kingsolver and Piercy fall into a category of feminist writers who make vivid and startling commentaries on how society views gender, but they—along with Margaret Atwood, for example—have no interest in voicing a unified feminist mantra that becomes mere dogma. In other words, the poetry of Kingsolver offers a feminist perspective, but she cannot be stereotyped in her messages. Kingsolver and Piercy challenge students even when they already feel sensitive to feminist issues—although these poems also serve as an excellent introduction to feminist perspectives for younger or less experienced students.

Issue-oriented poetry is quite valuable as sources for student writing. Students can use these literary experiences to write a wide range of original work. They certainly can be assigned fairly traditional analytical essays that show how Kingsolver or all three poems mentioned above raise similar questions about perceptions of female beauty. In addition, students can be assigned nonfiction essays that deal with a topic inspired by the poems but not directly with the poems themselves. And, of course, students may experiment with poetry themselves—exploring free verse, maintaining a unifying motif, manipulating popular trademark names, arguing issues of sexism.

Confronting Rape through Poetry

"[U]ntil some language was invented, Kingsolver was left to her own despair," writes Wagner-Martin (2004) about Kingsolver's rape in 1974 (p. 37). From that experience, Kingsolver produced the poems "Refuge" (dedicated to a woman raped by immigration officers before being deported) and "This House I Cannot Leave" (a poem of her own empathy for those violated). These two poems are stark in their wider and more personal politics, but such poems are important elements of our literary explorations because these topics remain unspoken far too often.

In "Refuge," students are asked to consider the abuses of those in power: The horror of the immigration and deportation situation in general is intensified by the rape. The poem has images of barbed wire and "a sharp blade" (1. 15) woven into the alluring voices of the immigration officers who represent the call of America for Juana. The second stanza has the officer "spread" the refugee's hand to find nothing, suggesting that he decides to take her physically since she has nothing to offer. The poem is disturbing in its content, but it also allows students to consider the faces of the growing number of immigrants who are at the center of America's rising anger at people who come to this country illegally. With this poem, we can ask students what Kingsolver seems to be implying in the poem of literal rape, with the final lines, "*the great/ desirability/ of my country*" (11. 25–27).

CONNECTIONS

The poetry of rape is shared by Marge Piercy's "Rape Poem" and Adrienne Rich's "Rape." These poems certainly can join a discussion of "Refuge" and "This House I Cannot Leave" as students begin to negotiate the use of literature and poetry to address both literal and figurative violations of women specifically and people more broadly. Piercy's poem directly faces the terrible violence of rape; her language is stark and vivid, and her style is direct, blunt. She also explores how the raped woman becomes the focus of accusations, how the raped woman can come to hate herself, to blame herself. The startling lines of the poem, "The rapist is your boyfriend's brother./ He sits beside you in the movies eating popcorn" (11. 16–17), make us acknowledge the fact that rape happens most often between those who know each other (a fact reflecting Kingsolver's date rape experience). Rich details the metaphorical rape by a police officer interviewing a rape victim: As in Kingsolver's "Refuge," "Rape" associates rape with an authority figure who feels no empathy for the violated woman, who frightens the victim of a crime. The woman raped in Rich's poem feels she is "guilty of the crime/ of having been forced" (11. 14–15).

"This House I Cannot Leave" begins with the speaker listening to a friend who has had her home robbed; eventually, Kingsolver reveals that the speaker understands too well being invaded, "thinking/ of the man who broke and entered/ me" (11. 21–23). This poem is similar to Rich's in that she uses rape both literally and metaphorically; it also echoes the psychological impact of the rape on the victim that Piercy details. With all of these poems, students should see the value and pain that come with expressing the fact of being raped. The poetry that grows from rape has many complex and disturbing qualities—anger, despair, confession, doubt.

CONNECTIONS

"I am nineteen, a grown woman curled like a fetus on my bed," begins one section of Kingsolver's "Letter to My Mother" (*Small Wonder,* p. 167). This is followed closely by a one-sentence paragraph: "I've been raped." This essay is about much more than being raped, but a central aspect is that Kingsolver is dealing with that rape both for herself and for her mother. The confessional letter, particularly to a parent or child, is fairly common in the literary canon. Kafka has a famous letter to his father, and Kingsolver also includes a letter to her daughter in *Small Wonder.* "Letter to My Mother" certainly fits this poetry unit on rape. We can have students read the whole essay or simply use the section discussing her rape. This essay reveals, as the poems do, the problems with reporting a rape and dealing with guilt; it also emphasizes the violence of rape. An interesting and challenging work that addresses conflicting perceptions of rape and date rape is Margaret Atwood's short story, "Rape Fantasies." This story can be added to this unit particularly for its disorienting tone and complex narrative technique.

Adrienne Rich (2002) and William Ayers (2001) have written often about the silence found in our classrooms; that silence is even more terrifying when it concerns the silence of victims. The poetry that grows from rape addresses the silences of our classrooms and the silences of our society. Kingsolver's own poems and essay can help bring her voice to the classroom and help raise our students' voices as well.

Approaching the Beasts—of Poetry and Nonfiction

"I donned the hard hat and entered the belly of the beast," Kingsolver (1995) writes in the essay, "In the Belly of the Beast," which includes part of her poem, "In the City Ringed with Giants" (p. 220). This essay along with her introduction to her collection of poetry provides a rich context for students to consider many contemporary debates about war and U.S. military history, to consider the nature of poetry and nonfiction, and to raise their pens in political expression. Kingsolver uses the beast image in both this essay and in her reference to poetry quoted at the beginning of this chapter. For our students, these multigenre lessons can help them face these beasts and discover their beauty.

"In the Belly of the Beast" and "In the City Ringed with Giants" spring from Kingsolver's own discovery of Titan missile silos ringing her adopted city of Tucson, Arizona. The essay discusses the chilling experience of visiting the silo-turned-museum that houses a deactivated Titan missile, and the poem was an attempt "to exorcise [her] nightmares . . . about the Titans" (p. 214). When students study this essay and her poem in conjunction, a number of varied and rich goals can be addressed, including:

- As an exploration of the qualities of vivid language in *all* writing, the essay and poem share similar craft elements—allusion, figurative language, manipulation of form and surface features (sentence and paragraph conventions in the essay; line and stanza formation in the poem), irony. These two works can serve as the source of a discussion of genre and effective craft strategies students need to recognize in their reading and implement in their writing. An interesting writing exercise is to have students deal with a single issue through both a poem and an essay—similar to Kingsolver. A secondary but important guideline for the assignment is to have students include similar craft strategies in each form.
- A unit revolving around these two works can also address large social problems that are relevant to young people. The essay and the poem raise serious concerns about war and peace, the history of U.S. military actions, the ongoing social debate about protecting the country through military buildup, the cycle of fear that is typified in Kingsolver's references to Cold War fears of the Soviet Union, and the right and responsibility of U.S. citizens to enter these larger debates. For young people, especially in the current culture of fear concerning terrorism, these issues remain relevant—particularly in light of Kingsolver's own admitted fear in her poem and her own somewhat eerie statement in her essay that "[o]ur leaders are hard-pressed to pretend some foreign power might invade us," penned many years before the 9/11 attacks on Washington, D.C., and New York City (p. 213).

CONNECTION

Two aspects of "In the Belly of the Beast" and "In the City Ringed with Giants" involve the fear of war or military attack and the gradual discovery of hidden history. These two works rely heavily on the sort of fear that grew out of World War II and the Cold War, a fear that centers on weapons of mass destruction (to use a term now in vogue). These works can be a link to an exploration of Kurt Vonnegut's *Slaughterhouse-Five.* In her essay, Kingsolver (1995) notes that during World War II, the United States became "the only nation that has ever used an atomic bomb" (p. 219). The ambiguity and irony of American might and

American love of freedom and peace as explored by Kingsolver are central to Vonnegut's own exploration of the infamous fire bombing of Dresden during World War II—an event in which Vonnegut found himself as a soldier, an event more devastating in terms of the number of people killed in the bombing than the atomic bombs used in Japan.

- These two works also fit nicely into more traditional aspects of the English curriculum. They are excellent starting points for lessons on mythology. These works play on allusions and references to the Titans of Greek mythology; more broadly, the essay forces the reader to consider the meanings of "myth" and "legend" as well as how the United States as a society functions within cultural myths that we rarely confront. A composition assignment that revolves around students exploring and describing the development of mythologies and legends within their own culture (music stars, movie stars, athletes) can grow from a classroom discussion of the meanings of "myth" and "legend."

ENTRY POINTS

As mentioned in Chapters Three and Four, Joseph Campbell and Bill Moyers' *The Power of Myth* is an excellent book (and video set) to help students connect the value of mythology and legend in their immediate life. "Maps and Legends," a song from an early album by REM, *Fables of the Reconstruction,* is a good entry point for discussing legends and mythology. The lyrics lead the listener to consider interpreting maps and legends, how we can become lost when we misunderstand.

As much as she challenges the reader to reconsider war, Kingsolver loves art, and the promise it offers in the face of doom. Her defense of teaching poetry in our schools opens her collection of poetry. This makes Kingsolver the poet and essayist an ideal source for what I have always found to be a highly effective guiding question while studying poetry: What makes poetry, *poetry?* In *Small Wonder,* Kingsolver (2002) expands the introduction to her collection of poetry as the essay, "Stealing Apples." This essay ends with her being inspired by her renegade child's disdain for math, feeling "when you find yourself laughing and crying both at once, that is the time to write a poem. Maybe that's the only honest living there is" (p. 234).

Kingsolver discusses poetry in the essay and mentions poet Lucille Clifton (whose work also resonates with students) to argue that poetry is not a foreign thing, that poets are people like any of us. The sentiments of her essay help us ask our students what makes poetry, *poetry,* and her arguments can offer a fertile setting for students to experiment with becoming poets themselves. For understanding poetry as a genre and for finding oneself as a poet, I have found focusing on the *unique element* of poetry highly effective. Whether I am teaching students to read or to write poetry, we come to agree that poetry is characterized by its concern for line and stanza formation as its guiding characteristic. Virtually all other tools at the disposal of poets are found in all the other genres as well. Growing in understanding of line and stanza formation is the most effective path to students embracing the genre. Line and stanza formation is a purposeful act of a poet. Reading Kingsolver muse about poetry in "Stealing Apples" and speak through her poetry supports students as they grow as readers and poets themselves.

The Languages and Cultures of Poetry

If Americans have found the world to be suddenly unsafe again—a new kind of Cold War raises its head in the form of terrorism—it has found that the voices and faces of America have changed as well. In both the introduction and the revised "Stealing Apples," Kingsolver (2002) declares that her collection of poems is her "testament to the two boldly different faces of America and the places I've found, or made or dreamed, in between" (p. 233). It offers our English classes, Spanish language classes, and courses for native speakers of Spanish learning English as a second language a unique and vibrant opportunity. *Another America/Otra America* is not only multicultural in its content but also bilingual, thanks to the Spanish translations by Rebecca Cartes.

Whether you are approaching multicultural or bilingual issues in your classroom, a good starting point is Kingsolver's "What the Janitor Heard in the Elevator." This poem from the opening section, "The House Divided," presents a self-incriminating dialogue between a "woman in gold bracelets" (1. 1) and her friend. Kingsolver raises issues of racism, of working-class immigrants, of language barriers—"Find another one that speaks English," the friend suggests (1. 13)—and materialism (gold jewelry, a broken vase). The poem also infuses the dialogue with loaded language—the woman in gold refers to the fired worker as "one" and the vase as "one"; she uses the word "worked" to mean "matched" as in the vase matching the décor. An added nuance to the poem is the title, "What the Janitor Heard in the Elevator," which implies both the apparent invisibility of certain types of workers, a janitor, standing in an elevator with the affluent women and the women's own lack of awareness of their racism and materialistic superficiality.

The poems of the second section, "The Visitors," then serve as a splendid means of dealing with multicultural issues that we face in American society today. "Refuge" speaks for Juana, a victim of rape by immigration officers. The next poem, "For Sacco and Vanzetti," continues Kingsolver's concern for often-ignored history and radical politics; it is based on a 1927 conviction of two innocent radicals (DeMarr, 1999). The final three poems of this section also have multicultural, historical, and political groundings. For students, these poems offer multicultural, historical, and bilingual experiences that are too rare in the traditional English curriculum.

CONNECTION

A natural and mirror-image companion to *Another America/Otra America* is the beautiful bilingual collection of poetry by Jorge Luis Borges, *Selected Poems* (2000), which includes stunning English translations by a number of notable poets. These poems from Kingsolver and Borges raise issues of language, of translation, and of cultures. Students who speak only English, students learning Spanish, and Spanish-speaking students who are learning English can all be brought together and brought into the world of poetry with the works of these two poets.

The bilingual nature of Kingsolver's collection offers a number of activities for students across a wide spectrum from traditional English students to English-speaking students learning Spanish to Spanish-speaking students acquiring English as a second language. In all these circumstances, activities dealing with translation are effective; some approaches include:

- An interesting source for pulling students into a consideration of languages is the debate over translation. An online search through amazon.com for Borges's *Selected Poems* includes recommendations by readers, a feature offered by amazon.com for most titles. For this bilingual collection, the comments revolve around the issues that haunt any attempt to translate from one language to another. These comments can be an excellent opening activity for students dealing with Kingsolver's poetry in both English and Spanish.
- Depending on the native language of the student, you can ask students to translate either the English or Spanish version of a Kingsolver poem from their nonnative language into their native language. After they have translated, either alone or in groups, students can compare their translations with those in the collection. Students begin to see the tension between literal and metaphorical language as that tension impacts basic translation and the doubly challenging task of translating the language of poetry.
- Naturally, students eventually try their hands at writing original poetry in both English and Spanish. This works best, often, as a brief

exercise where students work within some parameters such as a prescribed stanza form or specific syllable count per line. Both the Kingsolver collection and Borges collection can serve as models for this exercise.

Within their lifetimes, our students have witnessed a shift in the composition of American ethnic minorities. The Latinos and Hispanics have now surpassed African Americans as the largest minority group. This shift has created great social, linguistic, and political tensions in our country that are only likely to increase. Kingsolver's poetic exploration of the two Americas can be an effective avenue to addressing this rising concern for our schools, our students, and our culture.

Confronting Students as Poets—Dropping the Apple on Our Students

In "Stealing Apples," Kingsolver makes a confession that warms my heart. As a poet myself, I have often said that poems seem to come to me, unbidden, and I have tremendous problems writing poems on command—whether the request comes from someone else or from my own wish to write poetry. This is a particularly profound dilemma for all assigned writing in English classes; it is exacerbated in regard to the writing of poetry, I believe. All writing that is assigned becomes tainted to some extent, but asking students to write and to experiment with many forms is a necessary evil of teaching writing. Though I empathize with Kingsolver's sentiments as a poet, I know that as a teacher that I need to ask student to write poetry.

That said, I am as cautious about template poetry writing as I am about template approaches to essay writing (Thomas, 2005). Although we must assign writing, we must avoid prescribing anything that is inauthentic, particularly with poetry. I have had great success in using poetry of engaging poets, notably Dickinson (Thomas, 1998), as sources of both content to explore and form to mimic. With Kingsolver as a guide, students can attempt poetry in these ways:

- *Writing poetry from dialogue*—using "What the Janitor Heard in the Elevator" as a model, students can write a poem that creates or recreates a dialogue to reveal something about the characters in the poem that the characters themselves appear not to recognize. Students can work with similar techniques used by Kingsolver, as well—picking details that are charged with implication (gold bracelets, vase), manipulating the double meaning of a word ("worked," "colors"), manipulating the vague nature of some words ("one"), repetition.
- *Writing poetry from historical events of news accounts*—from "Beating Time" to "Deadline" to "For Sacco and Vanzetti," Kingsolver's

poems show students that poetry springs from the stuff of history and news. Students can often begin their poetry by reading interesting historical accounts or simply scanning several newspapers. Kingsolver sometimes includes a direct quote from the news or historical source of her poem; students can mimic that technique, further linking the connection they have explored earlier between poetry and nonfiction.

- *Writing poetry in traditional forms*—poets of all kinds swim occasionally in the structured poetry we often associate with the classic poets; Kingsolver includes in her collection a sonnet, "Portrait." Students vary in their responses to attempting highly structured forms. I tend to see asking students to write a sonnet as an *exercise.* Kingsolver's poem may be more accessible than a Shakespearean sonnet for many students and may make the form more relevant since she is a contemporary writer.
- *Writing poetry as a discovery and expression of Self*—a motif that runs throughout Kingsolver's work is a discovery of Self, and for her that discovery has multicultural roots. In "Naming Myself," Kingsolver explores the power of naming, the power of language, along with the discovering of Self through an exploration of ancestry. The poem shows Kingsolver working through her Cherokee ancestry and her wrestling with the traditional renaming of women when they marry. For students, writing a poem of Self that engages them with their family roots proves to be a valuable writing activity and a personal reward as well. "Naming Myself" works well as a sample poem in an activity such as the one suggested by Jago (2001) with Sandra Cisneros' "Abuilta Who."
- *Writing poetry from allusion and mythology*—as discussed earlier, "In the City Ringed with Giants," Kingsolver weaves a poem about nuclear missiles with allusions to the Titans of Greek mythology. Students who look closely at mythology often find sources for poetry much as they do with digging into history or news. Asking students to link an allusion to mythology to a current event proves to be an effective poetry activity.

Toward the end of the introduction to her collection of poetry, Kingsolver comes to her own rejection of the title "poet," but she concedes a passionate truth: "But when I want to howl and cry and laugh all at once, I'll raise up a poem against the darkness" (p. xix). When we bring Kingsolver's poetry into our classrooms to enhance their lives as readers, as writers, as humans we are sharing with them a passion that is at the heart of everything worth doing. Reading Kingsolver fulfills

Adrienne Rich's plea, "*You must write, and read, as if your life depended on it*" [italics in original] (1993, p. 32), a plea we must repeat endlessly for all whom we teach.

Another America

I. The House Divided

"Beating Time"
"Deadline"
"What the Janitor Heard in the Elevator"
"Reveille"
"Street Scenes"
"Waiting for the Invasion"
"*Justicia*"

II. The Visitors

"Refuge"
"For Sacco and Vanzetti"
"The Monster's Belly"
"In Exile"
"Escape"

III. The Lost

"American Biographies"
"This House I Cannot Leave"
"Ten Forty-Four"
"Portrait"
"Family Secrets"
"For Richard After All"
"The Loss of My Arms and Legs"

IV. The Believers

"Bridges"
"Naming Myself"
"Apotheosis"
"Orang-*Outang*"
"Ordinary Miracle"
"Babyblues"
"Daily Bread"
"Watershed"
"Possession"
"Frankfort Cemetery"
"Poem for a Dead Neighbor"

V. The Patriots

"Our Father Who Drowns the Birds"
"On the Morning I Discovered My Phone Was Tapped"
"The Middle Daughter"
"In the City Ringed with Giants"
"The Blood Returns"
"Remember the Moon Survives"
"Your Mother's Eyes"

ENTRY POINTS AND CONNECTIONS

"since feeling is first," e. e. cummings
What Is Found There: Notebooks on Poetry and Politics, Adrienne Rich
"Ourselves or Nothing," Carolyn Forché
"The Eye," Sharon Olds
"Storm Warning," Adrienne Rich
Walt Whitman
Lucille Clifton
"Barbie doll" and "A Work of Artifice," Marge Piercy
Anne Sexton
Sylvia Plath
Adrienne Rich
Pleasantville (movie), Director Gary Ross
"Rape Poem," Marge Piercy
"Rape," Adrienne Rich
"Letter to My Mother," Barbara Kingsolver
"Rape Fantasies," Margaret Atwood
Slaughterhouse-Five, Kurt Vonnegut
The Power of Myth, Joseph Campbell and Bill Moyers
"Maps and Legends," REM

Conclusion

Confronting Reading, Learning, and Teaching through Kingsolver

Since I could not do *everything* in this book, I hope that I did something well, as Thoreau suggests. One novel of Kingsolver's that I adore is *Animal Dreams,* but it has been somewhat ignored in the previous pages. I had to make choices.

In that novel, Codi returns to her childhood home and takes a job as a science teacher. In one scene, she explodes in front of her students, "What you people learn for a test you forget the next day. That's bullshit. That's waste of your brains and my time" (p. 254). Later, she is discussing with Loyd, her lover, his work as a train engineer. While Loyd is explaining the idiosyncratic nature of driving the train through a mountain pass, Codi asks him, "'Nobody can just tell you how to do that hill?'" And Loyd responds, "'No, because every train's different on every hill. Every single run is a brand-new job. You have to learn the feel of it'" (p. 295).

I love *Animal Dreams* because the scenes capture perfectly how I feel about teaching, how I feel about *telling* other people how to teach. This book is my attempt to give teachers and readers and even students fertile fields within which to grow as they need, as they see fit. I do not know each teacher who will read this, and I cannot know all the students those teachers will face. All of those factors matter a great deal; they matter more than anything I could tell some teacher to do with the works of Kingsolver.

So I offer this as an argument—bring the works of Barbara Kingsolver into your classes and the lives of you and your students. And I offer this as support for those acts. The conversation above between Codi and Loyd continues:

> "So you can't necessarily do the same thing next time?"
>
> "Not exactly the same thing, no."

Exactly.

Appendix
Confronting Pedagogy and Educational Psychology

Critical Pedagogy

The critical teacher works against what Freire (1993) calls the "banking concept" of teaching and learning. Freire argues that traditional educational thought sees learning as a passionless transfer of knowledge from the teacher to the student. As an example, let's begin with how we tend to treat literature and students in a traditional approach to *The Scarlet Letter.* Students are assigned the novel; some read part or all of it (though most do not actually read it, possibly reading a summary or nothing at all), and then the teacher spends several class periods telling students what they need to know about the novel—characters, plot, literary technique, and themes. Students are ultimately asked to give back to the teacher the interpretation the teacher gave to the students.

As Freire's metaphor aptly captures, knowledge is seen as mere capital that is deposited from some authority into some passive repository. Critical pedagogy rejects this view of teaching and learning as dehumanizing—and not authentic teaching and learning at all. In place of this limited view of education as transmission of knowledge, the critical classroom values meaningful dialogue, empowerment, consciousness/awareness, praxis, Marxist perspectives, Feminist perspectives, anticolonial concerns, and racial/cultural tolerance.

For both teachers and students, a culture of silence is at the center of personal, academic, and professional paralysis. When schools are not literally silent (which they often are), they are dominated by casual talking (that has no direct academic purpose—such as students or teachers sharing with peers or each other the details of their lives outside of school) and by talk directly *at* people but not a part of constructive dialogue. I believe schools comprise four kinds of talk and silence:

- Constructive talk—dialogue among everyone in the teaching-learning process in a nonthreatening environment.
- Constructive silence—listening that occurs by choice either within a dialogue or during a setting where one or several people speak without an opportunity for an audience to respond.
- Disengaged talk—talk directed *at* people within a threatening or coercive environment or within a casual environment.
- Disengaged silence—passive silence within a threatening or coercive environment, a state of silence that simply complies with a request to be silent.

As a critical educator, I see schools dominated by disengaged talk and silence, and I set as a goal of my course to move the class to constructive talk and silence. These types of talk and silence must be directly addressed within a classroom, and the distinctions must be carefully monitored (avoiding the blanket command "Be quiet," for example).

The critical classroom and the critical school encourage dialogue among all involved in the teaching-learning process—students, teachers, administrators, staff, and parents. Of course, dialogue requires all involved to speak, to listen, and to reflect on both. Dialogue is a complex process that at the very least creates a more complex set of ideas and perspectives than before the dialogue took place; ideally, dialogue creates action and even change. One element of the preceding chapters was how to implement literature as a source of dialogue for the teacher and the student.

The banking concept of education and the culture of silence in our schools are direct reflections of the failure of American education to confront issues of power. Teachers are often treated as technicians; someone in authority (by the nature of the position—regardless of the qualifications of the superior or the subordinate) prescribes what the teacher is to do and often how to do it: "Make sure these students pass the state assessment of reading and writing by correlating your objectives to the state standards and by matching your assessments with those same standards." The critical school environment brings everyone together to confront unrealistic and misguided mandates as a community to ensure that the primary goals of education are valued although schools have some legally binding obligations that may work against those higher goals. *Just because federal and state mandates require some misguided practices does not mean that they should be allowed to dictate the essential nature of a school.*

While this authoritarian model often leaves teachers feeling disempowered and dehumanized, those same teachers tend to turn around and treat their students in much the same manner—transmitting their knowledge to students and requesting that knowledge back within the parameters of the teacher's mandated template. Again, when teachers fall into this trap it is often as a result of top-down requirements that the teachers face themselves; that the oppressive nature of school trickles down, though, does not excuse the practices. If we confront literature as teachers and ask our students to do the same, we can use that literature to gain our own and our students' empowerment through the power of writing that Kafka treasured. Literature can work against the paralyzing nature of bureaucracy and authoritarian paradigms.

A first step to such journeys to empowerment through literature is gaining a new consciousness, a new awareness of Self and of the world. Especially when teachers and students see their actions as technical work, both teaching and learning deteriorate into somewhat mindless (ironically) tasks that are lifeless and fruitless. Literature provides a platform for teachers and students to step back from those mechanical actions, to deconstruct the assumptions of what they do. Once teachers and students begin to see things again for the first time, they can them begin to resynthesize how they think and what they do, central acts for empowered teachers and students.

Critical pedagogy embraces a concern for praxis, which is action driven by reflection. All of these elements within becoming a critical teacher or a critical student soon reveal themselves to be interrelated, thus inseparable. This holistic and chaotic nature, as I will discuss later, is also in contrast to the traditional habits of analysis and sequencing in our schools. We will emphasize throughout the following chapters that literature leads to praxis—although school often reduces literature and texts to sources for mere testing. A teacher is successful if she coerces the student into recalling the correct details from *A Tale of Two Cities* (along with correctly identifying the author). But *that* is not an authentic study of literature. It devalues literature and dehumanizes teachers and students.

Again, critical pedagogy embraces a series of concepts that are chaotically inter-related:

- Critical pedagogy rejects the banking concept of education, viewing the teaching-learning process as more complex than a transmission of knowledge.
- Critical pedagogy strives to supplant the culture of silence in schools with dialogue that foster constructive talk and constructive silence.
- Critical pedagogy seeks awareness and consciousness as the broad

goals of education, rejecting the reduction of teaching and learning to mechanistic functions.

- Critical pedagogy supports the empowerment of everyone through education.
- Critical pedagogy fosters praxis, action through reflection, infusing education with a moral component—social justice.

These qualities, as the following chapters will show, are essential components of authentic explorations of literature as well. Beyond these goals, these concerns, of critical pedagogy, the critical classroom will expand the limited perspectives and assumptions of the English classroom.

Our schools primarily reflect our society. As a result, schools function under many social assumptions related to capitalism, limited gender roles, and a wide spectrum of middle-class values. Teachers and students should use the study of literature in a critical classroom to confront those assumptions, providing Marxist, feminist, and anticolonial lenses to both teachers and students as they deconstruct the world through text. While the terminology and concepts may sound and feel dangerously confrontational, we will explore how these *perspectives* are essential parts of the teaching and learning process when the goal of education is the empowerment of teachers and students as integral parts of a democracy.

Let me offer a personal example to begin our discussion. A defining moment for me—a man who grew up in the late 1960s and into the 1970s when Twiggy, Goldie Hawn, and Farrah Fawcett defined feminine beauty as disturbingly thin—was learning that classic painting and sculpture reflected a *different* perspective of beauty. There was a time when pale skin and what would now be considered excess weight designated wealth in contrast to the drawn look of hunger and the tanned skin of working outdoors (qualities that were prerequisites of beauty in the 1960s and 1970s). I learned that *beauty was relative;* I learned that evaluations *could be* or more accurately *were* relative—not rules handed down by God.

Perspective, then, means everything. Too often in our English classrooms, in our quest to be objective, we proclaim objectivity through relative guidelines. Without a critical perspective, teachers and students fall prey to this contradiction. Although we have a long tradition of not allowing novices to move beyond objective evaluations of ideas and literature, the truth is that all literary reactions are drawn through a range of perspectives. Further, many writers themselves tend to express ideas that are grounded in the same critical perspectives we need to foster in our classrooms—Marxism, feminism, anticolonialism, and racial/cultural tolerance.

For many teachers and most students in America, our skewed and reductionistic views of terms such as "Marxism," "communism," and "socialism," adding a Marxist perspective to the critical classroom poses many relevant concerns. First, as teachers, we must have a clear understanding that all this means is that

- A Marxist perspective views literature through a lens that considers how the text explores and reveals issues of social class.
- A Marxist perspective views literature through a lens that sees history as a continual struggle for power.

Once we understand the central concepts, we have to ensure that students understand that a Marxist perspective for viewing the world and for viewing literature does not necessarily equate with being a political communist; as teachers, we must be sure that students set aside their misguided and corrupted perspective of Marxism, communism, and socialism, that students develop a nuanced understanding of a Marxist perspective as a valuable tool for raising one's critical awareness.

The feminist perspective as a central component of critical pedagogy carries some of the same concerns. Increasingly, the more conservative members of America have corrupted the term "feminism." A feminist perspective confronts the traditional balances (or imbalances) of power between males and females as well as between heterosexuals and homosexuals (and bisexuals).

Particularly in our post-9/11 world where the United States has taken preemptive military action, a concern for colonialism has regained significance for developing a critical perspective. The holistic and interrelated nature of this discussion raises its head again here. An anticolonialist perspective addresses power and the balances of power. Literature often personifies the dynamics of power on the large scale, exposing the dominance of one country or one culture over another.

Though it is difficult and somewhat artificial to name these perspectives, a final critical perspective is racial/cultural tolerance. A powerful characteristic of the American psyche, part of the middle-class mentality of schools, is that American culture is not simply different from other cultures, it is *better.* Racial and cultural tolerance views the races and cultures of the world as different but not necessarily better or worse.

Postformalism

Both from our experiences as students ourselves and from our direct training as teachers, we hold many assumptions about what teaching and learning are—with very little reflection or doubt raised concerning the process. While we come to see those assumptions as natural, they are actually anything but. One dominant view of teaching and learning has gradually become institutionalized in American education over the past century although many have argued that it may not be an accurate model of teaching and learning and certainly may not be the best model for students in a democracy.

The literature discussion throughout this book confronts the traditional assumptions of educational psychology, offering teachers an opportunity to reconsider the narrow and somewhat artificial assumptions of both behaviorism and constructivism in order to move toward a teaching and learning environment that embraces critical constructivism within a broader paradigm, postformalism (Steinberg, Kincheloe, & Hinchey, 1999). Now, let's confront not just our pedagogy but also the concepts and theories behind why we teach and how we believe people learn—the field that envelops teaching, educational psychology.

I have argued elsewhere (Thomas, 2004) that Americans have an odd love affair with capitalism, science, and quantifying; in our educational system, behaviorism, positivism, and quantification are institutionalized (through the momentum of tradition) and codified (through federal legislation, NCLB). Before we as English teachers can shift the practices of our classrooms to embrace postformalism (and as an act *of* postformalism), we have to identify and deconstruct the existing assumptions of the dominant educational psychology *in practice* within our educational system, within our schools, and within our classrooms.

Some argue that behavioristic psychology joined with assumptions about objectivity and quantification (the scientific process) to win the fight for dominance in the specialized field of educational psychology, holding a corner of the larger field of psychology that holds similar assumptions (Kincheloe, 2005). We will call the current state of institutionalized assumptions about teaching and learning "mechanistic" to capture a wide range of practices that work hand-in-hand to create the ways we teach and learn in traditional school settings. The mechanistic nature of schools—which we confront through our literature study—has grown from the work of Watson, Skinner, Pavlov, Thorndike, and others, whose names are quite familiar to those of us trained to teach. Mechanistic schooling practices these assumptions:

- Behavioral psychology is the best—and possibly only—theory of learning. Assumptions about stimulus/response drive lesson planning, assessment, and classroom management (including discipline).
- Western and American perspectives are the correct perspectives, borne out by the economic and military dominance of the West and America in the modern world.
- Teaching and learning must be driven by a narrow form of scientific research that embraces quantification of behaviors and the generalizability of empirical data. Educational research must seek

issues of causation and must verify those findings in strict lab situations that allow control groups.

- Knowledge is easily and objectively categorized into bodies of content that can be imposed onto students through the teacher as an authority. The best process for that teaching and learning is analysis, breaking bodies of knowledge into discrete parts and organizing those parts into linear models to be learned. This process also raises the efficiency of the teaching-learning process.

Most, if not all, of us understand this system well; it is a description of most of our experiences as students and teachers. These mechanistic qualities of schooling also work within a culture that embraces the consumerism and competition models of capitalism, that values entering the work force as a primary goal of schooling, and that embraces rationalism and cognitive processes over the emotional. Traditional schooling is a culture of analysis and quantifying—parts of wholes and numbers.

While few would argue that this mechanistic view of teaching and learning is not the dominant view, some have over the past several decades argued that the mechanistic approach is terribly flawed. Constructivism emerged as an alternative to behaviorism, and some have begun to explain that constructivism's grounding in Piaget has failed to move far enough out of the shadow of narrow views of scientific study, suggesting a critical constructivism, or more broadly, postformalism.

Just as the chapters in this book explore literature through critical pedagogy, they will also ground the discussion in postformalism (as a confronting of mechanistic assumption of teaching and learning). Since the purposes of this book and series are primarily concerned with teaching literature in high school and college, I will not take the time and space to debate the transition from constructivism (Brooks & Brooks, 1999) to postformalism, but I do want to establish how postformal thinking confronts the mechanistic nature of schools. Postformalism has its roots in the works of Piaget, Vygotsky, Dewey, Rogers, Bruner, and Howard Gardner—although the perspective is by its nature confrontational, everevolving, and both self-reflective and skeptical of the ideas it rejects and the ideas it embraces.

Kincheloe (2005) explains how postformalism looks in the classroom this way:

> Thus, in the spirit of John Dewey and Lev Vygotsky postformalism is about learning to think and act in ways that hold pragmatic consequence—the promise of new insights and new modes of engaging the world. In this context students in postformal schools encounter bodies of knowledge, not for the simple purpose of committing them to memory but to engage, grapple with, and interpret them in light of other data. At the same time

> such students are confronting such knowledges they are researching and interacting with diverse contexts. They are focused on the process of making meaning and then acting on that meaning in practical and ethically just ways. (in press)

With this broad context in mind, let's look at the nature of postformalism (and narrowly, critical constructivism):

- The scientific process moves beyond the quantitative to the qualitative. The traditional concerns for generalization, for lab settings, for control groups, and for causation are replaced with an interest in describing (language replaces numbers) authentic experiences in their natural contexts. The objective nature of reality is rejected for a relative nature of reality and truth.
- The teaching-learning process is seen as holistic and chaotic. Breaking content into parts and forcing those parts into a sequence are seen as both artificial and contradictory to brain research that shows most people to be global, not analytic, thinkers.
- The primary goal of education is to enter a democracy—not to enter the work force. Democratic values become the focus of teaching and learning, driving instruction, assessment, and classroom management.
- The center of the classroom shifts from the teacher and the content to the student. Learning is viewed as an inside-out process; a learner *constructs* meaning in unique and hidden ways through experiences with content, teachers, peers, and living.
- Literacy is highly valued as central to authentic learning. Dialogue is seen as essential for literacy empowerment and as a primary quality of a democratic classroom and a democratic society.
- The affective (how teachers and learners *feel*) is valued along with the cognitive (how teachers and learners *think*).
- The classroom becomes a place to consider issues of power, issues of oppression, issues of social justice, and issues of emancipation.
- All knowledge and all teaching-learning are subjective and contextual. Social, political, and cultural dynamics cannot be set aside from education.

A central confrontation of this book will be showing and asking teachers to use literature as an avenue for changing how they and their students see education and ultimately the world. For me, shifting the English classroom away from mechanistic practices and toward postformal groundings better fulfills the nature of literature (and art) and certainly addresses the dignity of students and the quest for democracy more fully than traditional practices. The postformal literature classroom embraces the passion that literature inspires.

References

Apocalypse Now Redux (1979). Dir. Francis Ford Coppola. Paramount Home Video.

Atwood, M. (1998). *Dancing girls.* New York: Anchor.

Ayers, W. (2001). *To teach: The journey of a teacher.* 2nd ed. New York: Teachers College Press.

Borges, J. L. (2000). *Selected poems.* Ed. Alexander Coleman. New York: Penguin.

Brooks, J. G., & Brooks, M. G. (1999). *In search of understanding: The case for constructivist classrooms.* Alexandria, VA: Association for Supervision and Curriculum Development.

Campbell, J., & Moyers, B. (1991). *The power of myth.* New York: Anchor.

Chopin, K. (1995). *The awakening and selected stories of Kate Chopin.* Ed. B. H. Solomon. New York: Signet Books.

Clifton, L. (2001). *Blessing the boats: New and selected poems 1988–2000* (American Poets Continuum series, Vol. 60). Rochester, NY: BOA Editions, Ltd.

Coleridge, S. T. (1991). *Poems of Samuel Taylor Coleridge* (Everyman's Library series, vol. 27). Rutland, VT: Everyman's Library.

The Complete R.E.M. Lyrics Archive. (2004). Available online: www.retroweb.com/rem/lyrics/index.html

Cronin, D. (2000). *Click, clack, moo: Cows that type.* New York: Simon and Schuster Books for Young Readers.

cummings, e. e. (1994). *Selected poems: e. e. cummings.* New York: Liveright.

DeMarr, M. J. (1999). *Barbara Kingsolver: A critical companion.* Westport, CT: Greenwood.

DeSalvo, L. (1996). *Vertigo: A memoir.* New York: Dutton.

Dewey, J. (1938). *Experience and education.* New York: Collier.

Dickinson. E. (1960). Hope is the thing with feathers. In T. H. Johnson (Ed.), *The complete poems of Emily Dickinson* (p. 116). New York: Little, Brown.

Ehrenreich, B. (2001). *Nickel and dimed.* New York: Metropolitan.

Emerson, R. W. (1981). *The portable Emerson.* New edition. Ed. C. Bode. New York: Penguin.

Endurance. (1999). Dir. Leslie Woodhead. Walt Disney Pictures.

Erdrich, L. (1984). *Jacklight.* New York: Henry Holt.

Forché, C. (1982). *The country between us.* New York: HarperPerennial.

Freire, P. (1993). *Pedagogy of the oppressed.* New York: Continuum.

Gandhi. (1982). Dir. Richard Attenborough. Columbia Tristar.

Gardner, H. (1999). *The disciplined mind: What all students should understand.* New York: Simon & Schuster.

Gardner, J. (1981). *The art of living and other stories.* New York: Ballantine.

Gardner, J. (1994). *On writers and writing.* New York: Addison-Wesley.

Hillocks, G., Jr. (2003). Fighting back: Assessing the assessments. *English Journal, 2* (4), 63–70.

Hughes, L. (1995). *The collected poems of Langston Hughes.* Ed. A. Rampersad. New York: Vintage.

Irving, J. (1996). *Trying to save Piggy Snead.* New York: Ballantine.

Jago, C. (2001). *Sandra Cisneros in the classroom: "Do not forget to reach."* Urbana, IL: National Council of Teachers of English.

Kafka, F. (1979). *The basic Kafka.* New York: Pocket.

Kincheloe, J. (2004). *Critical pedagogy primer.* New York: Peter Lang.

Kincheloe, J. (2005). Introduction: Educational psychology—Limitations and possibilities. In J. Kincheloe & R. Horn, eds. *Educational psychology: An encyclopedia.* Westport, CT: Greenwood.

King, Jr., M. L. (1986). Letter from Birmingham city jail. In J. M. Washington, ed. *A testament of hope: The essential writings of Martin Luther King, Jr.* (pp. 289–302). San Francisco: Harper and Row.

Kingsolver, B. (1998). *Another America: Otra America.* Trans. Rebecca Cartes. New York: Seal.

Kingsolver, B. (1988). *The bean trees.* New York: HarperPerennial.

Kingsolver, B. (1995). *High tide in Tucson: Essays from now and never.* New York: HarperPerennial.

Kingsolver, B. (1989). Homeland. In B. Kingsolver, *Homeland and other stories* (pp. 1–22). New York: HarperPerennial.

Kingsolver, B. (1993). *Pigs in heaven.* New York: HarperPerennial

Kingsolver, B. (1998). *The poisonwood bible.* New York: HarperPerennial.

Kingsolver, B. (2000). *Prodigal summer.* New York: HarperPerennial.

Kingsolver, B. (2002). *Small wonder.* New York: HarperPerennial.

Kingsolver, B. (1995). The spaces between. In B. Kingsolver, *High tide in Tucson: Essays from now or never* (pp. 146–157). New York: HarperPerennial.

Lindquist, T. (2004). Why and how I teach with historical fiction. *Scholastic.* Retrieved July, 13, 2004, from http://teacher.scholastic.com/lessonrepro/lessonplans/instructor/socia11.htm

Mabry, L. (1999, May). Writing to the rubric: Lingering effects of traditional standardized testing on direct writing assessment. *Phi Delta Kappan, 80* (9), 673–679.

Momaday, N. S. (1977). *Way to Rainy Mountain.* Albuquerque: University of New Mexico Press.

Myers, L. J. (2004). Memoir reflections: Writing and therapeutic healing. Memories and Memoirs. Retrieved July 13, 2004, from: http://www.memoriesandmemoirs.com/memoir_reflections.shtml

Oates, J. C. (2002). *Where are you going, Where have you been?: Stories.* Princeton, NJ: Ontario Review.

O'Brien, T. (1990). *The things they carried.* New York: Broadway.

Olds, S. (1984). *The dead and the living.* New York: Knopf.

Pawell, E. (1984). *The nightmare of reason: A life of Franz Kafka.* New York: Farrar, Straus, Giroux.

Piercy, M. (1994). *Circles on the water: Selected poems of Marge Piercy.* New York: Alfred A. Knopf.

Plath, S. (1981). *Sylvia Plath: The collected poems.* Ed. Ted Hughes. New York: Book-of-the-Month Club.

Pleasantville. (1999). Dir. Gary Ross. New Line Cinema.

Poe, E. A. (1988). *The portable Poe.* New York: Penguin Books.

REM. (1986). The flowers of Guatemala. *Lifes Rich Pageant.* Retrieved July 1, 2004, from http://www.retroweb.com/rem/lyrics/songs_TheFlowersofGuatemala.html

Rich, A. (2002). *Arts of the possible: Essays and conversations.* New ed. New York: W. W. Norton.

Rich, A. (1984). *The fact of a doorframe: Poems selected and new 1950–1984.* New York: W. W. Norton.

Rich, A. (1993). *What is found there: Notebooks on poetry and politics.* New York: W. W. Norton and Company.

Ryan, A. (1997). *John Dewey: And the high tide of American liberalism.* New York: W. W. Norton.

Scheele, A. (2004, May 6). The good student trap. *Washington Post.* Retrieved May 10, 2004, from: http://www.washingtonpost.com

Sexton, A. (1981). *The complete poems: Anne Sexton.* Boston: Houghton Mifflin.

Snodgrass, M. E. (2004). *Barbara Kingsolver: A literary companion.* Jefferson, NC: McFarland.

Steinberg, S. R., Kincheloe, J. L., & Hinchey, P. H., eds. (1999). *The post-formal reader: Cognition and education.* New York: Falmer.

Thomas, P. L. (1998). "It beckons, and it baffles—": Resurrecting Emily Dickinson (and poetry) in the student-centered classroom. *English Journal, 87* (3), 60–63.

Thomas, P. L. (2004). *Numbers games: Mandating and measuring American education.* New York: Peter Lang.

Thomas, P. L. (2005). *Teaching Writing Primer.* New York: Peter Lang.

Thomas, P. L. (2003). When choice failed—Or did it? *English Journal, 92* (3), 17–19.

Thoreau, H. D. (1975). *The portable Thoreau.* New York: Penguin.

Vonnegut, K. (1969). *Slaughterhouse-Five.* New York: Delta.

Wagner-Martin, L. (2001). *Barbara Kingsolver's* The poisonwood bible*: A reader's guide.* New York: Continuum.

Wagner-Martin, L. (2004). *Great writers: Barbara Kingsolver.* Philadelphia: Chelsea House.

Williams, W. C. (1991). *The collected poems of William Carlos Williams: 1909–1939, Vol. 1.* New York: New Directions.

Zinn, H. (1990). *Declarations of independence: Cross-examining American ideology.* New York: HarperPerennial.

Zinn, H. (1995). *A people's history of the United States: 1492–present.* Rev. and updated ed. New York: HarperPerennial.

confronting the Text, confronting the World

Bringing Writers into the Classroom

This new series in Peter Lang's education list will feature volumes that focus on one writer whose works are suitable for English classrooms at the high school and college levels. These books are a blend of introductions to the authors and their works, critical interpretation, explorations of best practice in reading and writing, and provocative considerations of learning theory and pedagogy.

Volumes will explore authors such as:

- Barbara Kingsolver
- Kurt Vonnegut
- Howard Zinn
- Margaret Atwood
- Clyde Edgerton
- John Irving
- Alice Walker
- Joyce Carol Oates
- J. D. Salinger
- Pat Conroy

For additional information about this series or for the submission of manuscripts, please contact:

Paul Thomas
[email] paul.thomas@furman.edu
Assistant Professor of Education
Furman University
3300 Poinsett Hwy
Greenville SC 29613

To order other books in this series, please contact our Customer Service Department:

(800) 770-LANG (within the U.S.)
(212) 647-7706 (outside the U.S.)
(212) 647-7707 FAX

Or browse online by series:

www.peterlangusa.com